# THE RULE OF EXPERTS

# THE RULE OF EXPERTS
## Occupational Licensing in America

S. David Young

CATO INSTITUTE

Copyright © 1987 by the Cato Institute.
All rights reserved.

**Library of Congress Cataloging-in-Publication Data**

Young, S. David, 1955-
 The rule of experts.

 Bibliography: p. 95
 1. United States—Occupations—Licenses.
I. Title.
HD3630.U7Y68     1987          351.82'43046          87-736
ISBN 0-932790-61-5
ISBN 0-932790-62-3 (pbk.)

Printed in the United States of America.

CATO INSTITUTE
224 Second Street SE
Washington, D.C. 20003

To Marvin Young

# Contents

|  | FOREWORD<br>*W. Clark Durant III* | ix |
|---|---|---|
| I. | INTRODUCTION | 1 |
| II. | A HISTORY OF OCCUPATIONAL LICENSING | 9 |
| III. | LICENSING AND THE PUBLIC INTEREST | 15 |
| IV. | THE DEMAND FOR LICENSING | 23 |
| V. | RESTRICTIONS ON ENTRY | 29 |
| VI. | LICENSING BOARDS: PROMISES AND FAILURES | 41 |
| VII. | EFFECTS ON INCOME AND COSTS | 49 |
| VIII. | LICENSING AND QUALITY | 53 |
| IX. | LICENSING AND OCCUPATIONAL MOBILITY | 59 |
| X. | LICENSING AND INFORMATION CONTROL | 63 |
| XI. | LICENSING AND INNOVATION | 71 |
| XII. | EFFECTS ON MINORITIES AND THE POOR | 75 |
| XIII. | PROFESSIONALS AND THE SCOPE OF PRACTICE | 81 |
| XIV. | THE REFORM MOVEMENT AND THE FUTURE | 87 |
|  | REFERENCES | 95 |

# Foreword

This is an important book. It addresses fundamental questions regarding economic freedoms. Under the pretext of ensuring quality control, occupational licensing in America restricts competition and choices for the ordinary consumer. It is a form of domestic protectionism, which, like all protectionism, ultimately harms the consumer. Higher prices, fewer choices, and less innovation prevail; economic freedoms are diminished.

It is not enough, however, simply to proclaim those truths, and David Young goes to great lengths to marshal empirical data that support such conclusions. Under occupational licensing, the heaviest burden falls on the poor. All of us are denied choices and opportunities, but the poor are especially burdened with higher costs and often must do without a particular service or commodity.

In my position as chairman of the board of the Legal Services Corporation, I see most acutely the impact of the lawyers' cartel on the poor. Along with the middle class, they are denied effective, low-cost dispute resolution services and legal assistance in part because of the laws protecting the legal profession. Occupational licensing permits that cartel to exist.

The legal monopoly rests on two major pillars. The first is the laws that set aside specific work exclusively for lawyers: the unauthorized practice of law (UPL) statutes. The second is the rules on how one may become a lawyer and what one may do after one becomes licensed. Like all such restrictions, they are really barriers to competition, not ensurers of competence, as Young's book, which touches on all the professions, explains.

Recently I went before the American Bar Association's Board of Governors to talk about these problems. I laid out in some detail the laws and rules that will need to be changed if our profession is serious about providing access to justice for all. Shortly after the conclusion of my remarks the president of the ABA called for my resignation, not for reform.

That reaction typifies what such organizations do to those who challenge them. Throughout the nation men and women who technically are not lawyers are trying to deliver legal services. The organized bar is trying to shut them down. In most cases it is not the clients that complain—they are well satisfied—but the bar, which does not want the competition.

Change ultimately comes about because of the power of ideas—the power of a shared vision. A proper understanding of David Young's work reveals a vision that would unleash the tremendous energies of a free and creative people and bring about an open and competitive system for the provision of services and commodities. The fruits of such a system would be lower costs and more opportunities for all. The Cato Institute deserves much credit for making Young's research available to the general public. As F. A. Hayek noted long ago, our political freedoms are very much connected to our economic freedoms. The loss of either leads to the loss of the other. Let the reforms begin—now.

—W. CLARK DURANT III
*Chairman of the Board*
*Legal Services Corporation*

# Acknowledgments

This book grew out of my doctoral research at the Colgate Darden Graduate School of Business Administration, University of Virginia. I am grateful to the members of my dissertation committee—Ken Middaugh, Whit Broome, and Mark Reisler—for their patience and guidance throughout the development of the project.

Others who provided helpful comments or advice on earlier drafts include Ken Elzinga of the University of Virginia, Benjamin Shimberg of the Educational Testing Service, and David Boaz of the Cato Institute.

Finally, I thank Bette Collins of the Darden School for her outstanding editing assistance.

# I. Introduction

> Any searching examination of privilege is unwelcome. Privileged groups are naturally aggrieved; from their point of view, privilege, once gained, is best forgotten. But, more generally, any critique of the professions must sound captious or ill-mannered. The professions operate in an atmosphere of almost sacerdotal reverence: the stillness of the courtroom, the antiquity of the solicitor's office, the embarrassed silence of the doctor's surgery. How unseemly to apply economic analysis to all that! But there are good reasons . . . even if it means stepping on corns that are sometimes ancient and always tender.
>
> —D. S. Lees[1]

Forming voluntary associations is a fundamental right in free societies. Physicians, attorneys, and other professionals are among those who have formed such associations in modern industrial countries. These professional associations have, quite properly, wide discretion over entry, expulsion, and the formulation of rules governing the conduct of their members. The major problem with this arrangement is the tendency for professional groups to impose these rules through state-enforced licensing laws. This particular form of government regulation—a pervasive characteristic of occupational groups in the United States—is the subject of this study.

A careful analysis of the effects of licensing across a broad range of occupations reveals some striking, and strikingly negative, similarities. Occupational regulation has served to limit consumer choice, raise consumer costs, increase practitioner income, limit practitioner mobility, deprive the poor of adequate services, and restrict job opportunities for minorities—all without a demonstrated improvement in quality or safety of the licensed activities. The evidence with respect to medicine, law, dentistry, and other highly visible professions is consistent with these findings. Indeed, some

---

[1]Lees (1966, p. 4).

of the most blatant and indefensible abuses of licensure have been committed by the most revered professions.

This study analyzes the economic, ethical, and political dimensions of licensure and reveals that, contrary to the assertions of professional groups, the public welfare is rarely advanced these laws.

**Professionalism in America**

Professional associations are largely a product of the extraordinary scientific, technological, and legal advances that have taken place since the Industrial Revolution. They reflect the demands of various groups in society for the existence of standards in an increasing variety of highly specialized services. Indeed, a modern nation without professions is impossible to imagine. By establishing minimal standards for, among other things, its members' education and training, professional associations help to promote the specialized skills that are highly valued by businessmen, consumers, and government agencies.

Professionalism in the United States generally refers to the provision of expert, high-quality service to consumers. Underlying this definition of professionalism is the assumption that professionals are granted the privilege of self-regulation in exchange for providing services at a fair price. Professions are granted autonomy from direct public control but are expected to give precedence to client interests over personal profit when conflict arises. In other words, professionals are charged with serving the public interest.

In accordance with this philosophy, professionals promote an image of their activities that they hope will distinguish them from other occupations. By tradition, professionals do not "sell" to "consumers"; they provide a service for "clients." Jethro Lieberman explains:

> The professional asserts that he is engaged in non-profit endeavor. The assertion is justified in part by the making of it, in part by noting that the basic charge is for time. Since there is no raw material to show a markup on, no profit can ever be visible.[2]

In theory, the client's welfare comes first; profits are secondary. In

---

[2]Lieberman (1970, p. 133).

addition, professionals are loyal to the group. They do not compete with colleagues by price-cutting or advertising, nor do they solicit new clients. As Lee writes, " 'Thou shalt not covet thy colleague's client' is perhaps the first commandment of the professional creed."[3]

Much has been written over the past few decades in an effort to define the term "professional" and delineate the differences between professions and other occupations. Most of the early work was done by sociologists using attribute models, that is, sets of attributes—"laundry lists," one might say—such that occupational groups that satisfied the attributes were considered "professions." Sociologists today are uncomfortable with this approach—a dissatisfaction that stems in part from the realization that the attributes are largely contrived and arbitrary and, more often than not, are devices for justifying forms of behavior (such as monopoly formation) considered inappropriate in other endeavors.

In addition, so many occupations satisfy at least some of the attributes that the notion of professionalism has lost much of its distinctive meaning. One might ask, for example, whether barbers are "professionals." Before industrialization only "learned" professionals—physicians, lawyers, and clergy—were considered professional. In the classic sense, then, barbers would not be considered professionals. Barbers do, however, display many attributes of professionalism as defined by sociologists, such as formal training programs, professional associations, the full-time nature of the occupation, and state licensing laws.

Sociologists have responded to the problems of attribute theory by developing continuum models. Even if certain occupations display characteristics of professionalism, the continuum model can demonstrate that they do not display these attributes to the same extent as other occupations and are, therefore, less "professional." Nevertheless, these refinements cannot avoid the inherent subjectivity and arbitrariness of the profession/occupation dichotomy.

An examination of the image learned professionals such as physicians and lawyers like to generate reveals that, contrary to the professional creed, such professionals behave much as those in other occupations. They do "sell" their services to consumers in exchange for money, just as do barbers, plumbers, or mechanics.

[3]Lees (1966, p. 7).

In reality, then, professionals are subject to the same forces of supply and demand as any other group.

Moreover, although professionals do not like to admit it, they well understand that mundane economic forces drive their activities just as they drive many other activities in society. This understanding is reflected in often successful efforts to impose artificial barriers to entry into the group. Professional groups know that, by reducing the supply of available practitioners, they can charge higher prices for services and, consequently, receive higher incomes.

This side of professionalism suggests something very different from the conventional view of a group dedicated to public service; it smacks of elitism, exploitation, and monopoly. Many citizens therefore view the professions as elitist groups responsible to no one but themselves and argue that, while professionals eschew economic gain in theory, they realize it in practice. This attitude is best reflected in George Bernard Shaw's famous dictum that "all professions are a conspiracy against the laity."

The controversy over the definition and nature of professionalism continues unabated. Accordingly, the terms "profession" and "occupation" often are used interchangeably. This alternation is much more than a stylistic device, however. It reflects a strong belief by many observers that the notion of professionalism obscures the true economic forces at work in the regulation of occupational activity.

### An Overview of Occupational Licensure

Most Americans know that practicing medicine without a license is against the law. They also know that lawyers, barbers, accountants, and dentists must have the state's approval before they can ply their trades. However, few Americans would guess that in some states falconers, ferret breeders, and eye enucleators are also subject to some form of government regulation. In fact, nearly 1,000 occupations are regulated by some or all of the 50 states.[4] The extent of regulation varies widely among occupations and across states. (While all states license the highly prominent professions such as law and

---

[4]Figures on occupations exhibiting various forms of regulation are from Greene (1983).

medicine, many occupations are regulated by only a few states and, in some cases, by only one.)

Understanding the extent and types of occupational regulation prevalent in the United States requires distinguishing among three levels of government intervention. The first and simplest form of regulation is registration, which usually requires little more of individuals than listing their names on official rosters. Any person willing to list his or her name has the right to engage in the given activity. Character references and bonding also may be required. Today 643 occupations in the United States require registration.

The next level of regulation is certification. Certification does not restrict anyone from engaging in a given occupation, but the use of certain titles is limited to those who have a certificate. Typically, an individual must meet certain qualifications to obtain certification. Requirements may include graduation from an approved training program, a certain amount of work experience, passage of qualifying examinations, and such personal characteristics as age, residence, citizenship, and moral character. At present 65 occupations are certified in at least one of the 50 states.

The third and highest level of occupational regulation is licensure, which requires that individuals obtain a license from the state to engage in a given trade or profession. Qualifications for licensure are usually similar to those required for certification. The key difference, of course, is that lack of certification does not bar someone from practicing the certified trade; it only prohibits him from presenting himself to the public as a "certified" practitioner. Licensure, on the other hand, prohibits practice without the license. At present 490 occupations are licensed in the United States; some occupations, however, may be licensed in some states but only registered or certified in others.

**A Challenge to Conventional Wisdom**

Until recently the growth of professionalism and the corresponding growth of occupational licensure were viewed benignly. From the beginnings of the modern professional movement early in America's history until the 1970s, professionalism proceeded with little opposition. That professionals restricted entry and restrained competition in their fields in order to serve the public interest was almost universally accepted. The possibility that such actions might be used to enhance professional income and power was considered to be, at worst, incidental to serving the public interest.

In 1945, however, Milton Friedman and Simon Kuznets published a study of the effects of professionalism on income. Although their research was the first to provide solid empirical evidence of the damaging nature of professional licensing laws, the study had little impact outside academia. Restrictive licensing laws remained in force throughout the post–World War II period and were even extended to include new occupational groups that had convinced state legislators of their "professionalism." The study did, however, set the stage for future work that was to alter radically the public debate on licensure.

No specific turning point marks the passing of the naive view of professionalism. Indeed, to this day many people, including professionals, assume that professionalism, although manifesting some abuses, does serve the public interest. Nevertheless, the intellectual journey from naive acceptance of licensure to skepticism about its social benefits can be traced through several events. One of the most important was the publication of Walter Gellhorn's *Individual Freedom and Governmental Restraints* (1956), the first work since the Friedman and Kuznets study to document the abuses of occupational licensing. In addition, Friedman's own *Capitalism and Freedom* (1962) devoted an entire chapter to the problems of licensure.

The establishment in 1958 of the *Journal of Law and Economics* at the University of Chicago was another important milestone. Until the late 1950s, all but a few social scientists viewed regulatory forces as benign (even if sometimes misguided), and regulatory activities were tacitly assumed to be costless. The journal served as a major outlet for a new literature on the effects of regulation—one that subjected many of the standard assumptions about regulation to rigorous investigation and found them wanting. Many scholars began to realize that government regulation was often a malevolent force restricting competition, raising costs to consumers, and indirectly transferring wealth to the politically powerful. Beginning with articles by Reuben Kessel (1958) and Thomas G. Moore (1961), many important studies of licensure have appeared in the journal.

The next major development occurred in 1971 with the publication of Chicago economist George Stigler's classic article, "The Theory of Economic Regulation." Stigler proposed a theory of regulatory behavior (known by various names, including the "economic," "capture," or "acquired" model) that was at odds with the traditional public-interest view. His model suggests that professional groups use the coercive power of government for their own economic advantage. In effect, they capture the regulatory apparatus and use it to restrain competition and raise income. An important implication of Stigler's theory is that regulation is enacted primarily because of political activity on the part of occupational groups, not because the public demands it. Social scientists have been somewhat frustrated in their attempts to model this theory formally, but much of the empirical evidence, as well as anecdotal evidence, lends credence to it as a plausible explanation of the regulatory process.

The consumer movement of the 1970s and its influence on federal regulatory agencies have also served to change public attitudes about professionalism. The result has been a slowdown in the growth of new regulation and, in a few isolated cases, the abolition of entire licensing boards. Some "sunset laws" have been enacted that require state agencies (including licensing boards) periodically to justify their existence or go out of business. Public representation on licensing boards has also become a popular way of improving accountability of these boards. In general, however, the results of the reform movement have been disappointing; most professional groups have so far succeeded in thwarting serious deregulation efforts.

## II. A History of Occupational Licensing

Scholars have traced regulation of the professions to ancient Babylon and the Code of Hammurabi.[1] Written about 1800 B.C., the Code set predetermined fees for surgeons' services and imposed penalties for malpractice (including the severing of a surgeon's hand if the patient died from an operation).

The first example of a licensing law similar to modern laws comes from 13th-century Sicily. Laws regulating the medical profession required prospective physicians to have extensive training (in philosophy as well as medicine), and provisions were made for testing candidates. All medical practitioners had to be licensed—a common feature today but nonexistent in those days. Fee schedules and ethical codes were established, and physicians were required to provide free service to the poor. In the next century, similar laws were enacted in Spain, Germany, and Naples.

The next major step in the history of occupational regulation was the ascendancy of the craft, merchant, and professional guilds of medieval times. These guilds, possessed of quasi-governmental authority, set prices and minimum quality standards and were also responsible for providing services to the poor and infirm. Guild regulation was similar in many ways to the modern-day system of regulation in which professional associations work in conjunction with government to enact licensing laws.

In general, the early guilds required membership of all who chose to practice a given trade or craft, thus creating a monopoly. High entry fees were often set, and consent of the guild membership was required before a new member could be admitted. This nearly total control over the trades permitted guilds arbitrarily to limit the number of apprentices that could enter the trade. Although at first the guilds were fairly open and restrictions were minimal, by the middle of the 14th century they systematically used their powers to restrict

---

[1]See Hogan (1979, pp. 223–24) on the early history of occupational regulation.

competition. In the next century, abuses became so rampant that economic growth was severely curtailed. Individuals who were unable to enter the guild system went into competition with guild members anyway. English courts in the 15th century began to challenge the monopoly power of the guilds by recognizing both the right of individuals to earn a living and the advantages of competition.[2]

The 16th century was marked by increased mercantilist practices that accompanied an expanding market, the accumulation of capital, the rise of powerful nation-states, and the emergence of the philosophy of laissez-faire.[3] All of these changes served to bring about further disintegration of the guild system. The centralization of authority common to this period also threatened the legitimacy of the guild system. In their bids for authority and revenue, monarchs demanded allegiance directly to themselves rather than to private social groups.[4] Thomas Hobbes and other leading theorists asserted that the state had sovereignty over its people. Intermediate groups, such as guilds, unnecessarily interfered with the "social contract" that allegedly existed between rulers and their subjects.

Frustrated by their efforts to achieve market control by private means, the English guilds turned to the state to secure enforceable monopoly privileges.[5] This process was repeated by governments throughout Western Europe, with the result that few could practice a trade without surmounting a battery of economic, social, and religious entry standards. The public had little choice but to pay exorbitant prices for the goods and services controlled by these legally enforceable monopolies.

The similarities between this system and the current licensing regime are striking. English authorities assumed that the chartered associations would use their monopoly power to ensure high quality and to discipline members for incompetence or fraud. The reality, however, was very different. Those granting state charters deferred to the expertise of the guilds in setting standards, which resulted in high prices, loss of economic freedom for non-guild

[2]Rubin (1980, p. 33).
[3]Hogan (1979, p. 224).
[4]Lieberman (1970, p. 41).
[5]The following four paragraphs are based on Rubin (1980, pp. 33–34).

members, and little or no improvement in product or service quality.

The English common law tradition alleviated some of the grossest abuses. The courts developed the doctrine that certain occupations have a special relationship with the public because of the critical nature of the service provided and the existence of a monopoly in its provision. From this doctrine developed the notions of "public callings" and "skilled callings," which imposed on monopolists an obligation to provide competent service to the public at a reasonable price. This doctrine was to have a profound influence on the development of regulatory law and professional litigation in the United States.

The Industrial Revolution, however, spelled the end for the guild system of public monopolies. The traditional guild structure eventually came to be seen as a serious constraint on economic growth, and the barriers erected by that structure were gradually torn down. Philosophical forces, most notably the publication of Adam Smith's *The Wealth of Nations,* accelerated the decline of guild franchises. Deregulation, however, was far from complete.

By the time the first American colonies were established, the guild system in Europe had already begun to deteriorate. For that reason, and others peculiar to the American experience, the guild system never took hold here. Seventeenth- and eighteenth-century America grew rapidly, with a corresponding growth in demand for the services of tradesmen, craftsmen, and professionals in a broad range of activities. Accordingly, the early Americans found European-style constraints on occupational activity unduly restrictive and contrary to the freedom and rapid rise in living standards that initially attracted them to America. One writer explains, "The land was open, the people pioneers, their goal adaption. To restrict the practice of any art to people specially trained would have been intolerable in a country where every man had to be . . . his own farmer, manufacturer, doctor, lawyer, builder, and banker."[6] Moreover, some regulatory constraints common in Europe, such as extensive education requirements and formalized apprentice programs, were not practical in the New World.

The first law regulating a profession in America was enacted in

---

[6]Lieberman (1970, p. 46).

Virginia in 1639.⁷ Its sole purpose was to control physicians' fees; other types of restrictions common to the European medical profession were not imposed. The first law enacted to control the *quality* of medical service was passed in Massachusetts ten years later. In the late colonial and early independence periods, individual states passed a variety of laws licensing physicians and surgeons. Gradually, state medical societies, under the domination of medical practitioners, began to take over the licensing function.

The early licensing movement met with considerable resistance, however. In the 1830s and 1840s, when the Jeffersonian/Jacksonian philosophy of laissez-faire was at its zenith, many consumers reacted negatively to state regulation of the medical profession. Their principal targets were state laws curtailing the operation of proprietary medical schools. Based on a firm belief in the doctrine of caveat emptor, reformers succeeded in preventing passage of licensing laws in several states and managed to have laws repealed in others. Consequently, by the mid-1800s the medical profession was open to almost anyone who chose to hang out a shingle.⁸

This state of affairs ultimately led to the formation of the American Medical Association (AMA) in 1847. Angered by what they saw as a proliferation of quacks driving down both the quality and price of medical care, the AMA's founders sought a powerful professional organization that would lobby for the interests of "responsible" practitioners—in short, tough licensing laws that would force poorly trained physicians out of the profession and provide a measure of economic security to those who remained. Although the AMA met with considerable resistance at first, its efforts eventually were resoundingly successful. By 1900 every state had enacted a mandatory licensing law.

In retrospect, the conditions that led to the formation of the AMA were not so bad as the leaders of American medicine believed. The deprofessionalization of the Jacksonian era not only stimulated the growth of medical schools and increased the number of doctors, but may also have raised the average level of standards.⁹ Rampant

---

⁷Hogan (1979, p. 225).
⁸Ibid., p. 226.
⁹Gross (1978, p. 1015).

quackery and deterioration of quality were taken as givens by the AMA's founding fathers, but the case was never proved.

Medical licensing laws afforded much more than simply economic protection. The history of medical licensure illustrates not only the enormous power bestowed on professional groups by regulation, but also how licensing has been used to eliminate, or at least curtail, the activities of unorthodox practitioners whether proven to be harmful or not. Throughout the early 20th century, the AMA used a variety of weapons to harass osteopathic physicians—branding them "cultist," denying them the right to practice in certain hospitals, opposing their recognition through licensure, barring them from local medical societies, and preventing medical doctors from associating with them professionally.

The AMA changed its position on osteopathy in 1961, primarily because of changes in the market for medical services. Specialization had become increasingly important in the medical profession during the post–World War II period, with the result that fewer and fewer AMA members felt threatened by osteopaths.[10] Because osteopaths are primarily general practitioners (GPs), they do not compete for patients directly with specialists and may even be an important source of referrals. Not surprisingly, the only serious opposition to recognition of osteopaths came from rural GPs who directly competed with them.

Of course, doctors were not the only professionals to lobby for extensive government licensing. Before the 19th century, a very few professions provided virtually all of the skilled intellectual services required by society.[11] The 18th-century lawyer, for example, performed functions that later would be assigned to such professional groups as accountants and real estate agents. Industrial development, however, fostered a division of labor that radically altered the nature of professional service markets. National associations representing various trades and professions began to proliferate in the late 1800s—a process enhanced by railroad expansion and improved means of communication such as the telephone and telegraph. This process accelerated during the Progressive Era as reformers relied on the presumed impartiality and knowledge of

[10]Rayack (1983, p. 152).
[11]Lieberman (1970, p. 43).

"experts." Through their state and local societies, these "experts" pushed through licensing laws at an ever-increasing rate: 110 statutes licensing 24 occupations were enacted between 1911 and 1915 alone.[12] Indeed, it appears that every organized occupational group in this country has tried at one time or another to acquire state licensure. Today as much as a third of the work force is directly affected by licensing laws.[13]

To conclude, the question of occupational regulation seems to have come full circle—beginning with the guild system, advancing to laissez-faire, then reverting to a guildlike system. In retrospect, however, this reversion is not surprising. Throughout history, competition has been viewed—correctly, it must be noted—as traumatic, disruptive, and unpredictable. A competitive economy may promote efficiency, innovation, and an increasing standard of living, but it is rarely comfortable. Accordingly, people will go to great lengths to protect themselves from competition. One common response has been the formation of guilds. The relative absence of guildlike behavior in the 19th century may be more of a historical aberration than the natural state of affairs.[14] In any event, the guilds are back. Comparing the current regulatory scheme with the guilds of the Middle Ages, Daniel Hogan writes:

> All of the elements of the guilds are present. Like the guilds, licensed professions have established the requirement of compulsory membership, creating a monopoly. Like the guilds, licensing standards have become higher and the cost of licensure has increased as educational requirements have lengthened. Like the guilds, periods of apprenticeship have been lengthened, the numbers of apprentices have been restricted, and in many cases the possibility of obtaining a license through apprenticeship has been eliminated.[15]

---

[12]Hogan (1979, p. 228).
[13]Ibid., p. 241.
[14]Benham and Benham (1978).
[15]Hogan (1979, p. 282).

# III. Licensing and the Public Interest

Occupational licensure is a form of government regulation and, like others, its principal justification is "the public interest." Regardless of the profession or trade, practitioners seeking new licensing laws or the toughening of existing ones always invoke the public interest: protection of public health, morals, or safety. In short, licensing is believed to protect consumers from incompetents, charlatans, and quacks.

A common argument made on behalf of the protective role of licensing laws asserts that regulation is needed to repair the market failure caused by consumers' lack of information regarding the quality of professional service. Sellers are specialized producers, whereas buyers are generally nonspecialized. Producers sell a small number of different commodities; households buy a large number of them. Given these differences, information is asymmetrically distributed; sellers know more about their wares than buyers possibly can.[1]

George Akerlof (1970) wrote the seminal work in this area. Although it does not deal explicitly with occupational licensing, his work clarifies the issues involved. Akerlof examined the market for used cars to point out the problems that can arise when a market is characterized by asymmetric information. He assumed that potential sellers know the quality of their own cars, while buyers have trouble distinguishing good cars from bad. He also assumed that buyers will know the general quality offered by the market but not the quality of any specific car. Because no one will pay more for one car that appears identical to the other cars, all cars of the same year and model will have the same price. The price, according to Akerlof, will reflect the average quality of those cars offered for sale.

Problems arise because owners of the highest quality cars do not

---

[1]Rottenberg (1980, p. 7).

find it worthwhile to sell at the market price, which reflects the low, average quality. When these sellers withdraw from the market, both average quality and price will fall. Owners of the next highest quality cars will then be induced to withdraw; price and quality will decline still further until, in equilibrium, only "lemons" will be offered for sale.

Hayne Leland (1979, 1980) formalized Akerlof's model and extended it to the case of occupational regulation. He argues, in a mathematically rigorous fashion, that while markets with asymmetric information will not always degenerate to lemons, some inefficiency in competitive equilibrium will occur. In other words, quality will be too low if left to an unregulated market.

The argument is as follows: In equilibrium, the marginal seller will find his opportunity cost just equal to the market price. Assuming that opportunity costs of the seller rise with quality, the marginal seller will always be of the highest quality level available for sale. The social value of a unit of the highest quality will exceed the social value of an average-quality unit. Yet the price received by the marginal seller is the same as the price received by all sellers, which reflects the average value in equilibrium. When this marginal seller offers his units for sale, average quality rises, and so does price. The high-quality seller must, however, split the benefits of this higher price with all other sellers. Because the marginal seller cannot have his units recognized as superior, he cannot receive payment for his full contribution to social welfare. According to Leland, this outcome drives a wedge between social and private benefits, resulting in low quality and inefficiency.

Leland considers some of the free market responses to this alleged market failure: seller guarantees, private information services, and retailer-provided quality screening services. While acknowledging the usefulness of such private arrangements, Leland finds fault with all of them.

Seller guarantees, he argues, are not voluntarily offered in many markets that exhibit asymmetric information. Private information services (for example, *Consumer Reports*) are confronted with the problem that, because information on quality has many of the aspects of a public good, it is underproduced. Leland views the third alternative, information intermediaries (for instance, retailers), more favorably, but finds fault here too. The retailer is motivated to monitor and maintain the quality of the products he sells because he knows that dissatisfied customers can shop elsewhere. However, information on the quality of sophisticated products—such as medical services or microwave ovens—may be difficult for retailers to assess. Moreover, many services do not lend themselves to distribution by middlemen.

Leland was therefore led to consider regulatory responses. He discusses three possibilities: payment of subsidies to suppliers, random restriction of entry to a fraction of suppliers (licensing on a random basis), and licensing based on minimum-quality standards. All involve government-imposed restrictions on individual behavior. The first involves the transfer of income through taxation and subsidies, while the other two place restrictions on market entry. The model shows that public welfare can be increased by all three if the market in question fits certain requirements.

Although Leland's model is the most rigorous defense of licensure, it has important weaknesses. The model's many simplifying assumptions contribute to its elegance, but the results are unrealistic. The first of these assumptions is the notion that government, through an omniscient social planner, can obtain information on practitioner quality without cost—a decidedly heroic assumption considering the complexity of the market for professional services.[2]

Another problem with Leland's model is the assumption that consumers are entirely ignorant of a supplier's quality, even though they are assumed to be completely knowledgeable about all *market* supply and demand curves. Whereas this assumption may have some limited validity for purchases of durable goods, it is irrelevant to the consumption of occupational services.

In addition, although consumers have less information on quality than producers, many information surrogates keep them adequately informed. They can acquire this information in several ways:

- By repeatedly purchasing certain goods or services;
- For infrequently purchased goods, by drawing on the experience of friends, relatives, and neighbors;
- From inferences drawn from the length of life of firms offering goods or services for sale; or

[2]Criticisms of Leland are based on Leffler (1980, pp. 288–90).

- For complex goods and services, from the sellers themselves, who have market incentives to provide consumers information on quality, often in the form of warranties.

One observer explains:

> Services of about the same quality are supplied continually over time by a particular supplier. Hence consumers will not face infinitely costly information; rather, they have some quality information from past experience and from friends, relatives, or information suppliers. This slight alteration in the model causes fundamental changes in the nature of free market equilibrium.[3]

Indeed, researchers have shown that, if consumers are able to check the veracity of suppliers *in any manner*, laissez-faire market equilibrium can support high quality.[4]

Of course, consumer knowledge can never be perfect. Information is a good that, like any other, is costly to produce. Rational consumers will therefore settle for a certain amount of ignorance. As Stigler explains, "There is no imperfection in a market possessing incomplete knowledge if it would not be remunerative to acquire (produce) complete knowledge; information costs are the costs of transportation from ignorance to omniscience, and seldom can a trader afford to take the entire trip."[5]

Government certification schemes also provide consumer protection. As with licensure, certification conveys a valuable quality signal to consumers, but certification is more flexible than licensure because it preserves free entry; only use of a title is restricted. Milton Friedman writes:

> The usual arguments for licensure, and in particular the paternalistic arguments for licensure, are satisfied almost entirely by certification alone. If the argument is that we are too ignorant to judge good practitioners, all that is needed is to make the relevant information available. If, in full knowledge, we still want to go to someone who is not certified, that is our business.[6]

Of course, we can go one step further toward a free market than

---

[3]Ibid., p. 290.
[4]Klein and Leffler (1981).
[5]Stigler (1967, p. 291).
[6]Friedman (1962, p. 149).

moving from government licensure to government certification: privately administered certification programs. Highly skilled practitioners have incentives to differentiate their product from the less skilled. Certification is one way to do this, and there is no reason why this function cannot be performed by nongovernmental organizations. In fact, many professional groups have done just that. Financial analysts, for example, have created the designation "Chartered Financial Analyst" (CFA) and have imposed rigorous entrance requirements to obtain it. Over 8,000 charters have been granted by the Institute of Chartered Financial Analysts, a private organization, since its formation in 1959. The designation has become so widely recognized in the investment community for its indication of high standards of ethics and knowledge that many employment advertisements for financial analysts specify applicants who are CFAs.

Finally, protection is given by tort law, which establishes the liability of sellers to compensate consumers for harm. Civil liability suits are the oldest and least interventionist response to quality breakdowns in professional markets.[7] If the negligence or incompetence of a professional causes harm to others, injured parties have recourse in a court of law. Providers are held to a standard of competence that generally prevails at a given time throughout the profession in question. Consequently, sellers have a powerful incentive to provide high-quality services.

One might argue that, even with the protections afforded in a free market, in certain cases notions of consumer choice are useless. For example, a person admitted to a hospital emergency room is unlikely to question the doctor's judgment. Even in this case, however, numerous constraints on professional abuse are present.[8] Peer pressure, patients' word-of-mouth, fear of malpractice suits, and the existence of alternative treatments all can serve to protect the consumer. Moreover, just because patients have little control over emergency-room care does not mean that they have no influence over routine care and thus need across-the-board protection in medical matters.

Therefore, despite assertions of Leland's model that quality levels

---

[7]Wolfson, Trebilcock, and Tuohy (1980, p. 191).
[8]Ibid., p. 192.

will be insufficient in markets characterized by asymmetric information, researchers have found that consumers cope quite well with such asymmetry. In relatively unregulated markets—those in which goods and services may be offered without constraints on entry or state-imposed quality standards—a broad range of products are offered for sale. Competition and free entry do not preclude the availability of high-quality goods and services. They are available (at relatively high prices) in many different markets, including clothing, housing, food, and various household goods.

As discussed above, justification for licensure comes from the notion that occupational service markets are characterized by information asymmetry; suppliers, by knowing more about the quality of their service than consumers, are able to manipulate consumers. The argument continues that, although unregulated markets may generate information that differentiates service providers along the quality dimension, and therefore mitigates the asymmetry problem, the information search can be very costly. Licensing, by increasing the relative supply of high-quality practitioners, reduces the information-search costs for those consumers who want high-quality service.

Consumers who prefer lower-priced, lower-quality service will be worse off with licensing, because such suppliers will not be permitted to practice. From a societal viewpoint, however, one can argue that it is economically efficient for licensing standards to be higher in areas where consumer demand for good quality is high. If consumers in some states demand higher quality than consumers elsewhere, the number of people made worse off as a result of licensure will be lower in those states than elsewhere.

Leffler (1978) tested this hypothesis with data on medical doctors. A proxy of quality was derived from information on the percentage of candidates taking a standardized national exam instead of the state licensing exam. The assumption was that a higher percentage of candidates in a given state would take the national exam if the state exam were more difficult than in other states. A further assumption was that the more difficult the state exam, the higher the state's quality standards.

Based on the assumption that quality of professional service is a normal good (that is, demand increases as income increases), Leffler proposed that consumers with high incomes would demand higher licensing standards than consumers with low incomes. And, indeed, that is what he found. In other words, the higher the consumer income in a state, the higher the licensing standards. This result, as well as results from other tests he performed, led Leffler to conclude that professional licensing (at least in this limited case) is based on consumer demand. His finding contradicts the widely accepted economic (or capture) theory of regulation. Although licensing advocates may take comfort from this evidence, an important fairness issue is raised.

The higher entry standards imposed by licensing laws reduce the supply of professional services, causing the market to clear at a higher price. In effect, then, the costs of the higher standards are distributed throughout the state in the form of higher prices. Affluent consumers who can afford these higher prices are better off, because the higher standards provide them with more confidence in the quality of the services they purchase. Poor consumers, however, do not benefit, because they cannot afford the higher prices. The poor are net losers, because the availability of low-cost service has been reduced. In essence, the poor subsidize the information-search costs of the rich. "The greatest good for the greatest number," perhaps, but the poor can hardly be expected to derive comfort from the argument that licensure, which makes them worse off as individuals, enhances social welfare.

# IV. The Demand for Licensing

> The declaration by a large number of different state legislatures that barbers must be approved by a committee of other barbers is hardly persuasive evidence that there is in fact a public interest in having such legislation. Surely the explanation is different; it is that a producer group tends to be more concentrated politically than a consumer group.
> 
> —Milton Friedman[1]

Crucial licensing decisions that can affect vast numbers of people are often made with little or no input from the public. Consumers are poorly represented at each of the key decision points in the licensing process: when a state legislature is considering a law to license a given occupation; when an already-licensed group is proposing rules and regulations that would determine standards for entry and professional practice; and when the legislature considers whether to continue or terminate a licensing board. Representatives from the occupational groups are always well represented at each of the key decision points, but rarely does anyone with a public-interest perspective testify.[2] If such a process serves the public interest, it is only by coincidence.

The political success of the professions at acquiring licensure is largely the result of the dynamics of small, well-organized, special-interest lobbying in the American political system. The fact that government regulation of the professions occurs mainly at the state level also plays an important part in this success.

**Interest-Group Politics and Licensure**

Public policy is heavily influenced by the political activity of competing interest groups. Lack of expertise among legislators and the fact that state legislative staffs are small and poorly funded

---
[1]Friedman (1962, p. 143).
[2]Shimberg (1982, p. 138).

mean that much of the information and analysis provided by interest groups would otherwise be unavailable to policymakers. Interest groups provide regulators with information and analysis that can, when properly used, serve the interests of the public. Naturally, however, each group takes positions and makes arguments that it regards as beneficial to itself. The policymaker's job is to sift through arguments based on self-interest and discover the valid arguments affecting the interests of consumers.

In the public-interest theory of licensing, regulation is introduced for the benefit of the public at the urging of consumers or their agents. Government is viewed as a benevolent, if sometimes misguided, body that seeks to maximize social welfare. Regulations are imposed at the urging of consumer interest groups because regulators believe, rightly or wrongly, that efficiency or fairness or both will thereby be enhanced.

Critics of this hypothesis believe to the contrary, however, that regulators' and professional groups' self-interest has been and still is the primary motivator of regulatory legislation. And indeed the evidence shows that consumers rarely engage in campaigns to license occupations. If the purpose of licensing were to improve the quality of service, one would expect consumers, who might be the prime beneficiaries, to promote licensure, but licensing is systematically promoted by practitioners. The reasonable conclusion is that the interests of practitioners are advanced by licensing laws. Of course, public and private interests may mutually benefit from special-interest lobbying, but the fact that the impetus for licensure invariably comes from professionals at least casts suspicion on the alleged public-interest nature of these laws.

In contrast to the public-interest theory is the economic model introduced by George Stigler, which suggests that government behavior in democracies is determined by legislators who are seeking to maximize their chances of re-election by responding to political pressure from voters, who, in turn, are seeking to use their votes to maximize their economic welfare. Whether a given regulation is enacted depends on the amount and type of political pressure different groups bring to bear on legislators, not on any objective criterion for social welfare.

Consistent with this model is the consideration of regulation, as with any other good or service, in a traditional supply-and-demand framework: interest groups demand it and politicians supply it. In terms of this framework, pressure groups "demand" regulation if they anticipate net gains from it. The "supply price" of getting a regulation enacted is the cost of the political action that must be undertaken to convince legislators.

This model is concerned with explaining why some professions have been more successful at securing favorable regulation than others and why professionals in some states have been more successful at political activity than colleagues in other states. What follows is a summary of research on the kinds of groups likely to be successful in the political arena.

*Group Size*

Groups with a small number of members tend to be better able to organize than groups with many members, primarily because small groups can more easily avoid the "free rider" problem. In any group, individual members have incentives to obtain the benefits of successful lobbying without bearing any of the costs, that is, to be free riders. In large groups, individual members can have difficulty perceiving that they have an important influence on the total effectiveness of the group, and thus need to do the work. The smaller the group, the greater is each member's share in the benefits realized by the group. Therefore, members of small groups are more likely to believe that group success depends on their own individual efforts. Also, small groups can more easily monitor the contributions of each member than can large groups, and thus are in a better position to apply peer pressure to members not contributing their fair share to the group efforts.

*Homogeneity of Interest*

The organization of groups whose members share a common, simply stated objective and have a similar stake in the outcome is likely to be easier and more effective than otherwise.[3] Homogeneous groups can devote all their time and money to the major issues they define. Efforts can be directed at legislators instead of to costly and divisive infighting.

---

[3]Noll and Owen (1983, p. 44).

*Self-Interest*

Participants in the regulatory process must have a reason for getting involved. Because the number of potential political and legal battles is large, people will tend to concentrate on those battles in which their personal stake is high. Economic factors such as the effects of regulation on prices and quality of service are likely to be major motivations.

One important measure of whether self-interest is a motivation for seeking regulation by an occupation is the per capita income of the occupation over time; raised income can be viewed as an indication of the probable reward of successful political action. Income may not rise, however, if demand falls. Thus, another aspect of economic self-interest as a motive for seeking licensure is that the value of licensing to a group depends largely on the price elasticity of demand for the occupation's services. Because licensure raises costs to consumers and, therefore, should lower the quantity demand, occupations facing inelastic demand (that is, those for which consumer demand is not highly sensitive to price) benefit the most from regulation.[4]

Licensure serves the economic interests of occupational groups because it can be used to protect group members from the inherent risks of free markets. In many areas of human activity, people purchase insurance policies to reduce risk. Given that many individuals have a substantial, undiversified investment in their professional education and training, it is hardly surprising to find a strong demand for human-capital or career insurance.[5] One way individuals hedge is by supporting institutional arrangements that function as insurance to protect members from market competition. Empirical evidence supports the argument that licensing results in greater income stability than in the general, unlicensed population. Jeffrey Pfeffer (1974) found that incomes in licensed occupations have been less correlated than general incomes with variations in median state income. In other words, licensed occupations seem better able to insulate themselves from local economic conditions. This factor

---

[4]Rottenberg (1962).
[5]Benham (1980, p. 14).

explains why professions are reluctant to accept removal of licensure even when regulation does not provide monopolistic returns.

*Opposition to Licensure*

If consumer or other groups believe they will be injured by licensure and find it feasible and profitable to oppose it, they can effectively increase the cost of obtaining it and thus weaken, delay, or even prevent the legislation. For example, hospitals have often used their clout to oppose licensure of certain health care professionals (other than physicians, of course) because of the higher operating costs that could result from such regulation.

## The Bias against Deregulation

Establishing licensure is only part of the story; its impregnability is the other. William White (1979) described why occupational licensure has dynamic and self-perpetuating effects on its own supply and demand once it is in place—the "escalator" effect and the "ratchet" effect. The former results in demands for more regulation once licensure is established, while the latter makes it more difficult to remove licensing laws than to block them initially. Escalator effects refer to the tendency common among all professions of increasing constraints on entry—for example, education, experience, and training requirements—after licensing laws have been introduced.

Ratchet effects occur when "grandfather clauses" permit incumbent members of the occupation to bypass the new entry requirements. Incumbents gain from licensing because licensing restrictions tend to raise the equilibrium level of wages above the free-market level as prospective members are kept out by the new entry requirements. It is important to note, however, that the gains to old members from entry restrictions are not immediate. They occur as entry restrictions gradually reduce the number of new practitioners. As White points out, there is no equivalent to grandfather clauses when *removing* licensing laws. If entry requirements are removed, new workers with lower qualifications can enter the occupation right away. Wages fall immediately, and everyone in the occupation loses regardless of whether they were licensed by the grandfather clause or by meeting the licensing requirements. Therefore, the *present value* of these immediate losses to incumbents is likely to be greater than the present value of gains from introducing licensure (which accrue gradually). Members of the occupation may thus be inclined to invest more in retaining licensing laws than in getting them introduced. This situation creates a bias against deregulation.

# V. Restrictions on Entry

> When the right to practice a particular trade or profession depends not on personal initiative but also on the approval of some agency, . . . the industry has laid the foundation for exercise of monopoly power. No longer may anyone perform legal, medical, accounting, architectural, or other tasks. The first condition for a competitive industry—freedom of entry—is gone.
>
> —J. K. Lieberman[1]

Because the major function of licensing is to prevent the unqualified from practicing, licensing is exclusionary. Those who meet a predetermined standard are licensed and allowed to practice; those who do not are excluded. Licensing laws generally require candidates to meet four types of requirements: (1) formal schooling; (2) experience, such as internships, apprenticeships, or supervised practice; (3) personal requirements, such as citizenship, residency, and good moral character; and (4) successful completion of a licensing examination.

The mechanism for enforcing these requirements and maintaining monopolistic control over a licensed occupation is the state licensing board. The state legislature, in effect, grants a charter to the board, and its members, frequently drawn from the regulated profession itself, are appointed by the governor. Many reasons have been given to justify this arrangement, including the importance of maintaining close cooperation between the state and the profession, the importance of ensuring competent, highly qualified board members, and the need for experts who understand the problems faced by practitioners.

An important weakness of this system from a public-interest viewpoint is that many requirements found in licensing statutes and enforced by licensing boards are there by dint of the practition-

---

[1]Lieberman (1970, p. 141).

ers' custom or some arbitrary choice, not because the public is really served by them. To illustrate, if a professional group suggests five years of experience as a requirement, a legislator is unlikely to raise the question of whether eight years, or four years, or less would be adequate.[2] Seldom are requirements based on careful analysis of what minimum levels of knowledge, skill, ability, and other traits are truly necessary to ensure adequate service. As a result, the impact of the requirements on practitioner competence has rarely been demonstrated.

Where, for example, are data supporting the notion that practitioners trained in different ways are dangerous? Andrew Dolan writes:

> Would most patients be in peril if physicians went to undergraduate school for two years instead of four and medical school for three years instead of four? How about 2.5 years of undergraduate school and 3.5 years of medical school? In nursing, where graduates of two-year, three-year, and four-year schools all qualify for taking state licensing examinations, the data do not indicate unacceptable performance among any of those groups.[3]

One excuse formerly heard in the medical profession for limiting entry was that letting too many people in would lower incomes to such an extent that doctors would resort to unethical practices to increase their income. But as Milton Friedman (1962) wrote: "This has always seemed . . . objectionable on both ethical and factual grounds. It is extraordinary that leaders of medicine should proclaim publicly that they and their colleagues must be paid to be ethical."[4]

Doctors are less inclined to make such assertions today, but their current entry-restriction practices, as well as other activities designed to limit competition in the health care field, suggest that professional attitudes have changed little over the years. Indeed, these attitudes have become especially apparent in the medical establishment's response to the so-called doctor glut crisis. Arnold Relman, editor of the *New England Journal of Medicine*, wrote:

---

[2]Shimberg (1982, p. 35).
[3]Dolan (1980, p. 37).
[4]Friedman (1962, p. 152).

> When there are too many physicians competing for too few patients, one can expect the ethical standards of medical care to be strained and the focus to shift from a primary concern for patients' needs to more preoccupation with the physicians' economic interests.[5]

This recent flurry of concern over the glut can be traced to a 1980 Graduate Medical Education National Advisory Commission study, which predicted a surplus of 90,000 doctors by 1990 and of 140,000 by 2000. As health-care economist Mark Pauly notes, however, the report was more political than technical: "[T]here is no scientific way of determining how many doctors we need, primarily because both physician productivity and the volume of physicians' services that could be absorbed in the treatment of disease are prone to change."[6] Indeed, as Pauly points out, the lower productivity of the increasing number of women doctors (because of fewer work hours per week and fewer years in practice than their male counterparts) has caused the Department of Health and Human Services to revise downward its surplus estimates.

Although Relman insists that the market will not adequately deal with the "oversupply" of physicians, Pauly suggests that it will and notes the recent experience of dental schools: Enrollment is down 23 percent today from its 1978 peak, with even further reductions expected. The decline can be traced to fewer applicants and not to the fact that dental school deans have been pressured into reducing enrollment. Apparently, Pauly concludes, "word got around that the market opportunities were drying up. . . . Assuming that the surplus [in medicine] is truly genuine, it does seem that medical schools could expect similar results."[7]

Another problem with entrance requirements is their potential for creating a snowball effect. Whenever some states increase standards for their professional groups, professionals in other states are liable to use the action as justification for higher entry standards in their jurisdictions. Benjamin Shimberg explains why: "No state likes to acknowledge its standards are lower, because this implies that its citizens are not as well protected as citizens of other states." Although the public may go along in the belief that more training

---

[5]Relman (1986).
[6]Pauly (1985).
[7]Ibid.

is always better, this type of thinking is fallacious. As Shimberg states:

> Beyond a certain point, additional training does not mean a higher quality of service. What it may mean instead is that the practitioner can charge more for his or her service because of the long time spent in training and because the supply of practitioners may have been thinned out by the unnecessarily long training requirements.[8]

**Problems with the Requirements**

In this section, the problems associated with the four types of requirements—education, experience, citizenship and residency, and licensing examinations—are briefly examined.

*Educational Requirements*

Educational requirements vary widely across professions; some require little formal schooling, while others require several years of post-graduate study. Schooling requirements in some professions, such as law, are at least partly justified because aspiring professionals learn their trade in postgraduate professional schools. The rationale, however, for ordinary educational requirements for trades that are not taught in high school or college is unclear. Why, for example, would states require beauticians to be high school graduates? Yet some do.[9]

The fact that educational requirements vary widely from state to state for the same occupation suggests the arbitrary nature of these provisions. The case of licensed practical nurses is instructive. Some states require only an eighth-grade education, some require completion of the tenth grade, and others require a high school diploma.

*Experience Requirements*

Experience requirements are common in the skilled trades, in which training tends to be highly job-related. The problem, however, is that requirements specified in licensing laws are often arbitrary, with time requirements for apprenticeship that bear little relationship to the actual amount of time needed to acquire minimum competence. Until the courts called a halt to it, for example,

---

[8]Both quotations are from Shimberg (1982, p. 40).
[9]Ibid., p. 36.

becoming a master plumber in Illinois took longer than becoming a Fellow of the American College of Surgeons.[10]

Another example of arbitrary experience requirements was found recently in Oregon, where the cosmetology board raised the number of training hours required for entry from 1,500 to 2,500 hours. Pressure for the change came primarily from owners of beauty schools, who could then charge more tuition and derive greater income from the services provided to customers in the schools' salons.[11] The effect has been to delay the entry of new beauticians into the job market by six months, at a cost to them of thousands of dollars in lost earnings.

A similar law was passed for barbers in Illinois. Apprenticeship requirements became so burdensome there that many candidates who would otherwise have completed their training simply dropped out and chose another line of work.

One could argue that the imposition of *any* experience requirements in most occupations is unwarranted. Completion of approved academic training and passage of rigorous examinations often reflect the same practical competence that candidates are required to demonstrate through years of documented experience.

The most systematic and complete study of experience requirements was performed by James Cathcart and Gil Graff (1978). They studied 58 occupations licensed by the State of California, all of which required passage of an examination for licensing eligibility. Twenty-nine of the occupations studied also had experience requirements.

To assess the need for experience requirements, Cathcart and Graff began with the impact of an occupation on the public. They developed a scoring system based on such factors as "seriousness" of impact; the higher the score, they argued, the stronger the case for experience requirements. Based on this scoring system, they found no rational basis for distinguishing between those occupations that required experience and those that did not. For example, funeral directors had no experience requirements, but embalmers were required to have two years of experience (including the disposition of at least 100 human bodies). Experience requirements for

---

[10]Gellhorn (1976, p. 14).
[11]Shimberg (1982, p. 39).

cemetery brokers were two years, but there were no requirements for cemetery salesmen.

In addition, they found no rationale for the length of required experience. Pest-control field representatives and construction inspectors received identical scores in the study, yet the former were required to have six months' experience, while the latter were required to have four to five years of experience.

Before granting a master plumber's license, New York City requires 10 years of journeyman experience—all of it under a master plumber in New York City. Many plumbers who have worked for plumbers in other states or for unlicensed contractors in New York City have learned that such experience could not be credited toward the requirement. As one critic notes:

> Such a rigid requirement—one that completely ignores the qualitative aspects of the individual's experience—appears to be more concerned with excluding "outsiders," no matter how qualified, than with assuring consumers that licensed individuals are safe and effective practitioners.[12]

In sum, experience requirements seem to be random and without any rational basis. Surprisingly, experience requirements have received few court challenges, even when such requirements appear arbitrary.

*Citizenship and Residency Requirements*

States often impose citizenship requirements on aspiring professionals. Many such requirements were passed in the 1930s as a xenophobic reaction to European refugees coming to this country during a time of job scarcity.[13] After Hitler came to power, there was a tremendous outflow of professional people, including physicians, from Nazi-dominated countries. Despite this migration, the number of physicians trained abroad who were admitted to practice in the United States in the five years after 1933 was the same as in the five previous years.[14] The threat posed by these foreign physicians led to a tightening of licensure requirements.

Recently the medical board in Tennessee grudgingly had to drop

---

[12]Ibid., p. 47.
[13]Gellhorn (1976, p. 14).
[14]Friedman (1962, p. 154).

a regulation that required foreign medical school graduates to have an education background *qualitatively* equivalent to that provided by AMA-approved schools in order to qualify for licensure. Because a foreign medical school accrediting agency did not exist, the regulation had the effect of barring foreign-trained physicians from practicing in the state. At a special meeting held by the state board to debate the issue, quantity seemed to be of more concern than quality. Former AMA president Tom Nesbitt told the board that, if the number of foreign doctors allowed to practice in the United States was not severely restricted, enrollment in American medical schools would have to be cut back. This statement prompted a Knoxville journalist to write, "In plain terms, what Nesbitt and [board chairman] John Burkhart advocate is nothing more than restraint of trade designed to insure that a glut of doctors doesn't affect their incomes like the oil glut has affected the price of crude."[15]

In March 1986 the New York state legislature sponsored hearings to investigate charges that the state unfairly restricted foreign medical school graduates from entering the medical profession. A staff report, "The Hidden Agenda: New York State's Restrictions on Foreign Medical Schools," cited recent state regulations as nothing more than an attempt to limit the number of doctors practicing in New York. The report noted that in recent years foreign-trained doctors have been disciplined less frequently than their American counterparts and that their clinical education is comparable.[16] The principal motivation for the numerical limits imposed on foreign doctors appears to be the predicted glut of physicians.

Defenders of citizenship requirements argue that for certain professions, especially law, the practice of the profession is so closely associated with the country's history and traditions that licensees should be citizens. Others say that a person who wants to practice a licensed occupation and enjoy the benefits that licensure bestows ought to become a U.S. citizen within a reasonable period of time.

The courts, however, have not accepted this line of reasoning. The rationale for overturning citizenship requirements is based on the Fourteenth Amendment, which provides that no state may deny

[15]*PRN*, August 1981, p. 6.
[16]*PRN*, February 1986, p. 3.

equal protection of the law to any person within its jurisdiction. Aliens, as well as citizens, are protected, and

> indeed particularly require protection, since aliens are a "discrete, insular minority" likely to be subject to prejudice and hostile discrimination. Therefore, state laws that cause aliens to be disadvantaged are highly suspect and can be justified only if the state can show that its differential treatment of aliens is necessary to satisfy a legitimate and important state interest.[17]

The courts have thus increasingly found citizenship provisions to be contrary to the public interest, and as a result of court challenges, a few such requirements have been revoked. For example, in 1981 a federal court declared unconstitutional a Louisiana law requiring a person to be a U.S. citizen in order to practice dentistry.[18]

In view of recent court rulings, citizenship may seem to be a dead issue in licensing, but this is not the case. Only some states have removed such requirements, and, where they are still in force, boards continue to list them as prerequisites to licensure.[19] So long as these requirements remain on the books—even when state attorneys general concede their unconstitutionality—aliens are naturally discouraged from applying for licensure.

Many states also require licensees to have lived in the state for a substantial period of time, although the relationship between prior residency and qualifications has not been established in any profession. Licenses also have been conditioned upon residency in jurisdictions smaller than a state. Plumbers in several states, for example, have prevented licensing on a statewide basis. Instead, licenses are issued by cities, which impose municipal residency requirements aimed at excluding outsiders from the local job market.[20]

As with citizenship requirements, however, many residency requirements have been revoked in recent court cases. An Alabama court, for example, found that a state provision requiring a candidate for the state bar to be a bona fide resident of the state was discriminatory and violated the privileges and immunities clause of the Constitution. The presiding judge charged that the rule fostered

[17]Shimberg (1982, p. 48).
[18]*PRN*, September 1981, p. 5.
[19]Shimberg (1982, p. 49).
[20]Shimberg, Esser, and Kruger (1973, p. 69).

"economic protectionism and parochial interest."[21] In 1985 New Hampshire's residency requirement for lawyers was declared unconstitutional by the U.S. Supreme Court. None of the reasons given by the state for refusing to admit nonresidents to the bar—they would be less likely to keep current of local laws and procedures, to behave ethically, to be available for court proceedings, or to do *pro bono* work—were deemed sufficient to discriminate.[22] In Florida a $1,000 license-renewal fee for nonresident doctors was recently ruled unconstitutional by a federal district court.[23]

As with citizenship rules, residency requirements appear to be unconstitutional, yet many remain on the books and continue to have an impact. Boards may continue to enforce them until challenged. Moreover, even if not enforced, residency requirements may have an intimidating effect on applicants. As Shimberg writes, "They may be deterred from applying for licensure in the belief that they will be turned down for failure to meet the stated requirement. This argues strongly for the repeal of all residency requirements."[24]

*Licensing Examinations*

One way for state licensing boards to determine the fitness of candidates is through a licensing examination. In some cases the board prepares and grades its own examinations, while in others it relies on national testing programs. Some states, for example, have their own bar examinations, while others use a multi-state exam. All aspiring certified public accountants take a national exam prepared and graded by the American Institute of Certified Public Accountants, a private organization. The scores are reported to each state accountancy board, which then decides, based on test scores and other criteria, whether to license the candidate.

The major technical problem in developing licensing examinations is to determine what abilities are critical for safe and effective practice of the occupation. Some argue that the principal criterion should be the relationship between certain abilities and client outcomes; that is, the decision to include a particular ability in a licensing exam should be based on evidence linking that ability to effects

---

[21]*PRN*, December 1981, p. 6.
[22]*PRN*, February 1985, pp. 5–6.
[23]*PRN*, March 1986, p. 5.
[24]Shimberg (1982, p. 51).

on clients.[25] The problem, of course, is that although some cases can rely on empirical evidence regarding the abilities/client outcome link (such as medical procedures based on clinical trials), this relationship is difficult or impossible to measure in many cases. What then?

The Uniform National Examination given to landscape architects illustrates some of the problems common to licensing examinations. A 1983 study conducted by consultants to the California Board of Landscape Architects found that fewer than half of the exam questions were critical to the protection of public health and safety. One subject, history, was found to have 40 nonjob-related questions out of a total 45 items. In addition, portions of the exam were found to test for *above* entry-level competence. In one section, only 58 of 90 questions were judged to be entry level.[26]

Given these problems, it may be tempting to rely on employment tests rather than licensing tests as a measure of a candidate's ability to perform in an occupation, but employment and licensing tests have major differences that should be considered.[27] Employment tests are designed to identify the individuals most likely to be successful on the job. In other words, their purpose is to predict job success. Licensing exams, on the other hand, should be designed to identify those who possess the knowledge, skills, and abilities to perform critical tasks in a manner that will adequately safeguard the public welfare.

Unfortunately, most licensing exams involve written responses to questions and extensive recall of a wide range of facts that may have little or nothing to do with good practice. For example, occupations such as plumbing and barbering rely on written exams devised by state licensing boards that test little more than the ability to memorize irrelevant facts.[28] Another example is the California licensing examination for architects, in which candidates are expected to discuss the tomb of Queen Hatshepshut and the Temple of Apollo.[29] The District of Columbia's cosmetology exam recently

---

[25] Kane (1982, p. 915).
[26] *PRN*, October 1983, p. 1.
[27] Shimberg (1981, p. 1140).
[28] Hogan (1979, p. 255).
[29] California Department of Consumer Affairs (1978).

required applicants to do finger waves and pin curls—styles that have been out of fashion for decades. Those procedures most likely to harm consumers—bleaching, coloring, and permanent waves—are not tested on the practical exam and receive little emphasis on the written exam.[30]

Even standardized national exams, now common in many professions, have failed to demonstrate anything more than superficial validity. Indeed, some critics have expressed amazement that important improvements in teaching methods developed since World War II could have so completely bypassed the field of occupational licensing.[31]

Perhaps the most significant criticism against licensing tests is the charge that grading standards have sometimes been manipulated to reduce the number of entrants in tough economic times. Elton Rayack's 1976 study for the U.S. Department of Labor provides evidence for this point. Rayack hypothesized that failure rates on licensing exams would tend to vary with the general or occupational level of unemployment. Evidence consistent with this hypothesis would indicate that licensing boards use the exam system to protect licensed practitioners from increased competition, especially during hard times.

Rayack found the relationship between failure rates and unemployment rates to be statistically significant for 10 of the 12 licensing exams he studied. For example, failure rates on electricians' exams in Massachusetts were significantly correlated with national unemployment rates for a 58-year period. The results indicate that nearly 15 percent of the variation in failure rates could be explained by changes in unemployment figures. The evidence from Rayack's study suggests that in certain circumstances licensing boards tend to fail a high percentage of licensing applicants, regardless of qualifications, in order to reduce the flow of new entrants into the market and thereby strengthen the competitive position of those already licensed.

Alex Maurizi's 1974 study provides further evidence on this point by testing the hypothesis that pass rates are a function of an occupational "queue." This queue was defined as the ratio of new

---

[30] *PRN*, December 1984, p. 5.
[31] Shimberg, Esser, and Kruger (1973, p. 194).

applicants in the state to the number of licensed practitioners already in the state. The greater this ratio, the greater the excess demand.

Maurizi tested data on pass rates and the occupational queue for 18 occupations as of 1940 and 1950. Although some of the occupations did not show a significant relationship between the two variables, when all occupations were combined, the predicted negative relationship was found to be highly significant. On average, a 10 percent increase in the queue generated a decrease in the pass rate of from 1 to 10 percent. In another test, Maurizi found that a 10 percent increase in average practitioner income produced up to a 10 percent decrease in the pass rate. He concludes:

> This evidence tends to confirm the notion that the power of licensing boards is often used to prolong the period of higher incomes resulting from increases in excess demand for the services of the occupation in question and that the instrument then used to accomplish this purpose is alteration of the pass rate on the licensing examination.[32]

---

[32]Maurizi (1974, p. 412).

# VI. Licensing Boards: Promises and Failures

> The great truth that is never spoken directly, but anybody in the field with two bourbons in them will tell you, is that these boards work primarily to protect the practitioners and have little or nothing to do with protecting the public.
>
> —Former Virginia state official[1]

Although the professions have met with some success in raising the general tone of professional conduct, the fact that experts often sit in judgment of themselves—conferring, suspending, and revoking licenses—raises the question of whether they sufficiently consider the public interest in their deliberations. The most frequent criticism lodged against licensing boards has been their failure to discipline licensees. A major cause is the reluctance of professionals to turn in one of their own. The in-group solidarity common to all professions results in members who frown on revealing unsavory activities of a fellow member to the public.[2] Going public regarding infractions, no matter how grievous, is often viewed as disloyalty to the professional community.

Although licensing agencies are entrusted with the responsibility of protecting the public from quacks, incompetents, and charlatans, they are usually more zealous in prosecuting unlicensed practitioners than disciplining licensees. In many occupations, complaints of malpractice usually are brought by licensed practitioners, not consumers, and these complaints become more common when economic conditions worsen.[3] Even when action is brought against a licensee, harm done to consumers is unlikely to be the cause; professionals are much more vulnerable to disciplinary action when they violate rules of competitive behavior. A 1986 report issued by the

---

[1]Isikoff (1983).
[2]Haug (1980, p. 66).
[3]Rayack (1976).

U.S. Department of Health and Human Services claims that, despite the increasing rate of disciplinary actions taken by medical boards, few such actions are imposed because of malpractice or incompetence.[4]

Evidence of lax disciplinary practices abounds. In 1972 only 0.1 percent of all practicing lawyers in the United States were subjects of disciplinary proceedings.[5] So few lawyers are punished, in fact, that many lawyers concede that the bar's enforcement machinery is ineffective at weeding out or disciplining unethical members. Formal sanctions do little to deter potential violators, because the most common violations receive only mild sanctions. In addition, most disbarments are by consent, and thus the record and charges are not made public.

One might conclude that only 0.1 percent of lawyers deserve disciplinary action, but consider the following: A recent survey of lawyers found that three of ten had witnessed judicial misconduct, but 58 percent did not report it.[6] Of those who failed to report, 29 percent said it was not worth doing because nothing would have happened anyway, 19 percent said it was not their responsibility, and 5 percent said they did not want to ruin another lawyer's career; the remaining nonreporters did not give a reason. According to the director of the American Bar Association's Center for Professional Responsibility, several other factors contribute to the low reporting rate. For example, lawyers may fear too much time would be taken testifying in a disciplinary proceeding, they may not know where to report the misconduct, or they may be afraid of being sued.[7]

The situation is similar in the medical profession. According to many doctors, the reason for the low incidence of disciplinary actions is that physician competence and ethical standards are high. There is cause for doubting this claim, however. One study estimates that 2 to 10 percent of all doctors are involved in unscrupulous, unethical, or incompetent activity.[8] This percentage translates into roughly 7,500 to 35,000 practitioners.

---

[4]U.S. Department of Health and Human Services (1986).
[5]Hogan (1979, p. 258).
[6]*PRN*, October/November 1985, p. 10.
[7]Ibid.
[8]Hogan (1983, p. 124).

A study conducted by a consumer health group noted that, of 400,000 physicians treating patients in the United States in 1983, only 563 had their licenses suspended or revoked or were placed on probation.[9] The study further reports that nine states and the District of Columbia reported no disciplinary actions to the Federation of State Medical Boards. Also, the state with the largest increase in malpractice insurance premiums in 1985, New York, had one of the lowest disciplinary rates in 1983. To illustrate the inconsistency of enforcement across the country, the rate of disciplinary action in Utah (the state with the highest such rate) was found to be 36 times higher than the rate for Massachusetts.

Although inadequate funding of state boards is often cited as a reason for poor enforcement efforts, one observer, Seattle attorney Andrew Dolan, suggests that inadequate funding is not responsible for the prevalence of incompetent physicians. He claims that the emphasis of medical disciplinary efforts on economic crimes rather than incompetence has been a major factor in the medical malpractice crisis.[10] When boards are confronted with malpractice cases, the disciplinary decision often turns on the political or personal characteristics of the targeted physician. "Therapeutic dissenters" (doctors with views that the mainstream of the profession finds threatening) are easier targets for licensing boards than incompetent doctors with less threatening personal views.

Dolan predicts that recent innovations in health care delivery, such as health maintenance organizations, may do more for countering the malpractice crisis than rigorous enforcement of licensing laws. Market incentives may induce such operations to root out incompetent doctors more quickly than conventional licensing-board enforcement efforts:

> Integrated health care systems have incentives to only hire competent people. . . . What is the incentive of a board member to address medical malpractice? In large measure it's a matter of personal integrity—but personal integrity is normally distributed throughout the population. . . . I think any system that is premised on personal heroics is doomed to failure.[11]

---

[9]*PRN*, July 1985, p. 5.
[10]*PRN*, September 1985, p. 2.
[11]Ibid.

States that are genuinely interested in addressing the prevalence of malpractice should encourage health care systems with the liability and marketplace incentives to keep the level of malpractice low, and the authority to move quickly against incompetent doctors without the bureaucratic burdens that beset licensing boards and professional societies. Dolan argues that the boards should continue to handle the most extreme cases of incompetence, but a private system of tort law and market incentives is necessary to ensure quality medical care "at the margin."

The evidence of disciplinary actions in other professions is no less disturbing than in medicine. A 1979 report observes that the New York State Department of Education, which licenses 450,000 professionals, disciplines fewer than 200 licensees per year. In California a 1978 report of the state's Regulatory Review Task Force confirmed that many boards lack the will to discipline incompetent or dishonest practitioners. The task force found that as much as 16 percent of the dental work performed in 1977 under insurance plans was so shoddy as to require retreatment. Yet in that year, the dental board disciplined only eight of its licensees for acts that had caused harm to patients.[12]

There is also reason to doubt whether licensing laws are a deterrent to charlatans. Evidence from the medical profession shows that many impostors have acted as physicians for long periods without being detected. And when detection does occur, often it is by accident.[13]

Furthermore, the study of medical history indicates that quacks flourish whenever physicians are scarce or when their remedies are ineffective. Licensing laws may actually worsen this problem by artificially restricting the supply of practitioners. Quackery also may be served if politically powerful fringe groups receive formal recognition through licensing laws.[14]

Problems with enforcement are widely acknowledged by both licensing officials and professionals, with most of the blame being placed on state legislatures for not providing boards with stronger

---

[12]Data for New York and California are from Shimberg (1982, pp. 101–02).
[13]Hogan (1979, p. 263).
[14]Friedman (1962, pp. 155–56).

tools with which to do their job.[15] Critics cite weak laws that often fail to give boards explicit authority to discipline licensees even for gross negligence, a limited range of sanctions, and inadequate resources for investigating and prosecuting complaints.

In a few states, reforms have been implemented that may improve the ability of licensing boards to protect the public. California now has a medical quality assurance board with a recently expanded budget and 45 investigators. Illinois set up a disciplinary board separate from the board that licenses physicians, with the result that the number of physicians losing their licenses has substantially increased. Twenty-nine states have sought to strengthen the enforcement process by granting immunity from civil action to physicians and other professionals who provide information on infractions to regulatory boards. Nine states have gone even further by requiring physicians to inform their medical boards about colleagues who fail to meet minimal standards of practice.[16]

While more licenses are revoked today than ever before, some recent cases suggest that in some states it may be impossible for a professional to commit a crime serious enough to ensure revocation. A Chicago lawyer who murdered his wife and was found innocent by reason of insanity eventually had his license restored after responding to psychiatric treatment. Three Massachusetts doctors convicted of rape were allowed to keep their licenses while their case was on appeal. A 1985 report of Ohio's Legislative Services Commission revealed that disciplinary sanctions of physicians were delayed when criminal penalties were involved.[17] Doctors awaiting felony convictions were allowed to continue practicing for several months or even years. The pharmacist and doctor responsible for giving Elvis Presley vast overdoses of drugs both kept their licenses.[18] The pharmacist had voluntarily surrendered his license but later had it restored.

Another glaring indication of licensure's ineffectiveness at protecting the public is the failure of various systems to reassess periodically a practitioner's competence. Laws requiring evidence of

[15]Shimberg (1982, p. 104).
[16]Ibid., pp. 112–13.
[17]*PRN*, December 1985, p. 5.
[18]*PRN*, November 1981, pp. 6–7.

continuing education (CE) have been adopted to remedy this situation. Typically, practitioners can meet the requirements by attending professional conferences or taking extension courses. Although CE requirements may appear to be an important step in shoring up the quality of professional service, the promise has proved greater than the reality. Moreover, the financial impact of CE programs on less affluent members of the professions raises important fairness questions.

Another problem is the difficulty of determining what constitutes an acceptable CE program. To illustrate, a 1981 study showed a wide divergence of opinion between practicing physicians and medical school professors who teach family practice on what kinds of CE courses need to be taught. Academics are accused of being too ignorant of practice problems, while practitioners may not be keeping abreast of current academic developments.[19]

Benjamin Shimberg's 1982 study of CE programs found that, while on the surface CE requirements ask a great deal of practitioners, in reality they demand very little. Weaknesses include insufficient resources and personnel to oversee mandatory CE programs, ambiguous grading standards, and the lack of evidence linking formal CE requirements to competence. The present system relies on the discretion of practitioners to select courses they believe to be most appropriate. There is no guarantee that practitioners will try to correct their weaknesses. Indeed, it is much more likely that they will select courses in their current areas of expertise, with the justification that, if a course must be taken, it may as well bolster expertise in a chosen area of specialization.

A review of CE programs in California revealed that four of the six state licensing agencies investigated had given licensees credit for inappropriate courses.[20] Examples include courses in memory skills and assertiveness training courses for accountants; public speaking, veterinary medicine, and banking courses for dentists; and a course in positive mental attitude for pharmacists.

A 1985 report of Washington State's Office of Financial Management charged that the state's mandatory CE program for psychologists does not accomplish its goal of ensuring that licensees main-

---

[19]*PRN*, September 1981, p. 7.
[20]Office of the Auditor General (1984).

tain a minimum level of competence.[21] The report recommended that either the system be strengthened to assure continued competence or the public should be informed that the state credential assures competence only at the time of initial licensure.

Self-assessment tests have been proposed as one way of assisting professionals in identifying their weaknesses, but such tests are now voluntary and few professionals use them. To require such tests and the subsequent correction of weaknesses as a condition for continued licensing would be tantamount to reexamination, a horrifying prospect to most professionals. In those few instances in which reexamination is required, the scope of coverage is very limited. Florida's accountancy law, for example, requires licensees to pass an exam before renewal of their licenses, but the material tested is limited to the state's accountancy law and the accountancy board's rules.

[21]*PRN*, December 1985, p. 2.

# VII. Effects on Income and Costs

Studies indicate that licensing restricts entry by imposing high entry costs; fewer people join a licensed occupation than would be the case in the absence of licensing. This outcome does not create shortages as such, but the market does clear at a higher price. Whether these higher prices translate into higher practitioner incomes depends on the price elasticity of demand—that is, the sensitivity of consumer demand to price changes. The more inelastic demand is, the more practitioners have to gain from reducing supply and raising prices. If the demand for a licensed trade is highly inelastic, the loss in revenue caused by lower demand will be more than offset by the increase in price. If, on the other hand, demand is highly elastic, a small increase in price will result in a large decline in consumer demand. What then does the evidence indicate regarding the effects of licensure on the income of those licensed?

Milton Friedman and Simon Kuznets (1945) were the first researchers to document the effect of occupational regulation on entry restriction and income. They found that the number of medical schools in the United States declined by almost one-half from 1910 to 1940, while the number of physicians per 100,000 population declined from 157 in 1900 to 130 in 1938. Similar results were found for dentists.

They concluded that differences between professional and nonprofessional workers' incomes seemed larger than necessary to account for the extra skill and training of the professionals. In addition, about half of the difference between mean incomes of physicians and dentists was caused by the greater difficulty of entry into medicine than into dentistry.

Since the Friedman and Kuznets study, many researchers using modern methodologies have found similar results. For example, William D. White (1978) examined the effects of licensure on wages of clinical laboratory personnel. He distinguished between two types of licensing laws, both mandatory but one more stringent than the other. The more liberal laws did not appear to have a significant impact on the wages of clinical laboratory personnel. The more stringent laws increased the relative wages of licensees by 16 percent in the two cities studied, Los Angeles and San Francisco. Based on his findings, White concluded that the immediate impact of recent licensing laws has been small, but the long-term impact of older, more stringent laws on wages has been substantial: "In the absence of any evidence that occupational licensure increases the quality of laboratory tests, the results for older, more stringent laws suggest that policy makers should be cautious in introducing new licensure laws or strengthening old ones; these actions may sharply increase costs and leave quality unchanged."[1]

Lawrence Shepard (1978) compared average fees for dental services between states that recognize out-of-state licenses and those that do not. Most states refuse to honor licenses granted in other jurisdictions. Dentists who seek to practice in those states must pass local examinations regardless of their previous experience. Given the nonstandardized and often irrelevant nature of many licensing exams, the requirement tends to constrain the supply of dentists and, hence, dental care. This practice also has the effect of insulating practitioners from the threat of competition from out-of-state dentists who might otherwise migrate.

Only 15 states in Shepard's study had reciprocity agreements binding them to endorse each other's licenses. The other 35 exercised their discretion to limit the immigration of dentists by failing a significantly higher percentage of nonresident new dental school graduates than the reciprocity states.

Shepard's sudy provides evidence that, where states have erected competitive barriers, dentists systematically charge higher fees than elsewhere. Controlling for other factors, he estimates that the price of dental services and mean incomes of dentists are 12 to 15 percent higher in nonreciprocity states. As of 1976 the annual cost to consumers of this form of professional control was approximately $700 million.

Surveys of professional attitudes reveal that dentists well understand how licensing affects their financial interests. Where fees are higher than average, dentists are more opposed to reciprocity agree-

---

[1]White (1978, p. 102).

ments than elsewhere. On the other hand, young dentists establishing practices and older dentists contemplating retirement are in favor of improved mobility.

Research based on Canadian data has yielded results similar to Shepard's. In 1980 Timothy Muzondo and Bohumir Pazderka studied the effect of advertising, fee-setting, and mobility restrictions on the earnings of 20 professional groups across 10 provinces. Adjusting across professions for differences in human capital (such as schooling), restrictions on advertising were found to increase earnings by nearly a third, while restrictions on fee competition increased income by more than 10 percent. Mobility restrictions had no significant effect on earnings.

Pazderka and Muzondo did a follow-up study in 1983 using a different methodological approach. They considered the effects of licensing restrictions on consumer costs and found that advertising and fee-setting restrictions each increased earnings by about 11 percent. Mobility restrictions were responsible for increasing professional income by over 4 percent. Taken together, all three types of restrictions enhanced earnings by nearly 27 percent. The aggregate cost in 1970 to Canadian consumers was found to be almost $350 million. Moreover, this figure underestimates the impact of licensing on income because it does not incorporate the effect of entry restrictions.

Licensure also often results in the misallocation of skilled labor and professional services. As Mancur Olson notes, the consequence of this misallocation to a country's economy can be substantial. The wealth transfers to occupational groups that often result from licensure are more damaging, dollar for dollar, than transfers to the poor. The poor are, on average, less productive than the nonpoor and are more likely to lack marketable skills or possess attributes that contribute to economic success. Conversely, people who are most productive and whose skills are highly valued by society tend not to be poor.

When the nonpoor, such as doctors and lawyers, are subsidized through cartelization arrangements such as licensing, their time and energies are channeled into less productive pursuits, thereby reducing social efficiency. Olson explains:

> Professional associations and public policies that largely control the practice of law and of medicine are no doubt . . . costly to the

society, because it is the time of some of the most highly educated and energetic people in the society that is being misallocated; yet few areas of modern society are so rife with cartels, anticompetitive rules, and other redistributions as are the law and medicine.[2]

---

[2]Olson (1986, p. 262).

# VIII. Licensing and Quality

Licensing laws are designed to assure the public that only competent people will be allowed to practice, and some evidence supports the argument that licensing restrictions enhance quality. In his study of optometry, for example, J. W. Begun (1981) derived a measure of quality based on the length of an eye examination, office equipment, and examination complexity. He found that more restrictive standards were associated with higher quality of service. Samuel Martin's (1982) study of pharmacists used the number of malpractice suits per licensee as a proxy for quality and found similar results.

Despite these studies, however, most of the evidence suggests that licensing has, at best, a neutral effect on quality and may even cause harm to consumers. By making entry more costly, licensing increases the price of service rendered in the occupations and decreases the number of people employed in them. Some consumers therefore resort to do-it-yourself methods, which in some occupations has led to lower overall quality and less safety than if there were no licensing.

To illustrate the failure of licensing to enhance quality, consider the Federal Trade Commission's (FTC) study of the relationship between licensing and fraud in the television repair industry. Incidence of fraud and misrepresentation was sampled in three locales: Louisiana, which licenses TV repairmen; Washington, D.C., which has no regulations; and California, which merely registers TV repairmen. The study found the incidence of fraud more frequent and prices 20 percent higher in Louisiana than in either of the other jurisdictions. The evidence suggests that licensure is not an effective way of regulating unethical behavior. The FTC study indicates that a better approach to encouraging honest service is to rig a few television sets with defects, then have government officials pose as consumers and take the sets to repair shops. The government can then prosecute those making unnecessary repairs. This approach, the study found, has significantly reduced unnecessary repairs.

A 1983 FTC study of contact lens fitting found little difference in the quality of service performed by opticians, ophthalmologists, and optometrists, despite large differences in price. Predictably, ophthalmologists are the most expensive providers, opticians and noncommercial optometrists next, and commercial optometrists the least expensive. (Commercial fitters are those who employ others, use a trade name, advertise heavily, and are located in retail stores; noncommercial fitters are in more traditional, solo practices.)

Despite the price differences, the quality of lens fitting in 500 wearers in 18 cities as assessed by the professionals themselves was the same among the three professional groups, as well as between commercial and noncommercial fitters. The study suggests that state laws, such as those that ban opticians from fitting lenses or that prohibit commercial practice, result in higher prices by limiting consumer access to lower cost providers. While the FTC believes that consumers can, by using commercial optometrists, save up to one-third of the cost of contact lenses without sacrificing quality, the American Optometric Association remains opposed to commercial practice and has conducted an extensive media campaign to convince consumers that private practitioners provide the best quality care.[1]

Fred S. McChesney and Timothy J. Muris (1979) even found an instance in which the *lack* of restrictiveness corresponded to higher quality. They compared conventional law firms with legal clinics in Los Angeles to test the effect of legal advertising on the quality of service. Based on surveys of clients, the study found that, despite charging lower prices, the clinics did not provide a lower quality of service. On some quality measures, the clinics scored better than traditional firms.

Sidney L. Carroll and Robert J. Gaston's (1981) examination of seven professions showed that, in each one, extensive restrictions were detrimental to consumers in all cases in at least some states. Furthermore, none of the professions demonstrated a significant relationship in the opposite direction. They found that houses tend to stay on the market longer where real estate brokers are tightly regulated and that the incidence of rabies is higher where there are strict limits on veterinary practice.

[1]*PRN*, January 1984, pp. 4–5.

In a later study, Carroll and Gaston (1983) point out that even if higher licensing standards do enhance practitioner quality, this fact does not guarantee that higher quality will be *received*. In other words, overall effectiveness of the service received by all consumers, whether served by licensed professionals or by substitutes, may decrease as licensing laws become more restrictive. Carroll and Gaston illustrate this point with a hypothetical model.

The service in question is interstate travel and the licensing restrictions apply to airline pilots. A hypothetical quality index is constructed:

$$Q = P^{10}/A$$

where Q is quality; A is the average time of all interstate trips in the society, whether by airplane or not; and $P^{10}$ is the probability of safe transit taken to the tenth power.

Enacting rudimentary licensing restrictions may significantly increase $P^{10}$ while holding constant (or even decreasing) A. For example, a screening device may be used to weed out psychotics and drunks; these restrictions would increase Q. However, as restrictions increase, diminishing returns set in on $P^{10}$ (are 2,000 hours of pilot flight time much better than 1,500?). Restrictions may lead to a substantial decrease in the number of pilots (as well as higher wages for those remaining and thus higher costs for consumers). Consumers as a group are induced to use slower, less costly substitutes for their travel needs. "As a consequence, Q eventually must fall as restriction increases, irrespective of the . . . effect on pilot skills."[2]

Although licensing is intended to limit entry to qualified people, it can generate other, perverse effects on the quality of service rendered. Licensing conveys a credential that signals a practitioner's competence to consumers. Incompetent practitioners who obtain a license, however, may be able to attract business that might have flowed to worthier competitors if the free market had been permitted to operate.[3] The normal checks exercised by consumers in a free market are substantially missing in a licensing regime because consumer judgment is supplanted by professional accreditation. In

---

[2]Carroll and Gaston (1983, p. 142).
[3]Barger (1975, p. 199).

short, licensing gives incompetents instant credibility even though they do not deserve it.

A study by Alex Maurizi provides an excellent illustration of this point. Maurizi examined data on consumer complaints (a proxy for quality) made to the California Contractors' State License Board and found that minimum competency standards for licensed contractors were being circumvented. The ratio of complaints to licensees increased during the period from 1954 (when the board began to maintain complaint files) to 1975. Part of this increase can be explained by the increased number of branch offices of the board, which made it easier for consumers to file complaints. Maurizi found, however, that the number of schools offering courses to help enrollees pass the contractors' licensing exam (together with the fact that the exam changed little from 1964 to 1975) was also a significant cause of more complaints. There were no such schools in 1964; by 1975 there were 57. Very simply, exam schools were making it possible for low-quality practitioners to circumvent the minimum-quality standards by teaching them to pass the exam without learning the skills of a contractor. Thus, Maurizi concludes, "Consumers may be receiving a quality of service quite similar to what would prevail in the absence of licensing, and they may be paying higher prices for that quality."[4]

The irrelevance of licensing in promoting the public safety is also evident in the case of radiological technicians. Congress passed a bill in 1981 that requires the Department of Health and Human Services (HHS) to develop certification and accreditation standards for dental hygienists and assistants and for radiologic and nuclear medicine technologists—all of whom perform procedures involving radiation. The standards are voluntary, but the HHS encourages states to implement licensing programs based on them.

The standards were promoted by the American Society of Radiologic Technologists and the American Dental Assistants Association and were supported by a growing public concern over the dangers of radiation overexposure. The case presented by dental assistants and radiologic technologists on behalf of licensing x-ray operators was, however, largely anecdotal. Moreover, evidence suggests that licensing is unlikely to have much effect on safety.

[4]Maurizi (1980, p. 34).

When the standards were enacted, 10 states had already prohibited people from operating radiologic equipment without some certification. A Food and Drug Administration study compared states with licensure to states without and found no significant differences in levels of radiation exposure; the study was unable to determine whether licensure enhanced or detracted from good radiation practices.[5]

In addition, critics pointed out that the federal bill did not even address the real problem in radiation exposure, namely, overprescription. The solution to this problem lies with physicians, dentists, and other health care professionals who prescribe x-rays. Yet the bill would have had virtually no chance of passage if it had been designed to regulate providers of primary health care. Physicians and dentists understandably resist all attempts to impose constraints on professional judgment.

---

[5]*PRN*, August 1981, p. 3.

# IX. Licensing and Occupational Mobility

Licensing laws can create maldistributions in the supply of practitioners, especially when laws make it difficult for licensed professionals in one state to obtain a license in another. Retirement states such as Florida might appeal to professionals who want to practice part-time, but those states are noted for the stringent and arbitrary requirements imposed on out-of-state professionals. Sunbelt states in general have experienced substantial growth in recent years, and they attract numerous out-of-state professionals. Worried by the migration of what it calls "snowbirds," the Texas medical board now requires out-of-staters seeking a Texas physician's license to take the third part of the exam sponsored by the Federation of State Medical Boards.[1]

Of course, geographical mobility would differ among professions even in the absence of licensing because of differences in earnings potential, education, age, and types of employment contracts.[2] Recent studies indicate, however, that the costs of mobility are higher when restrictions are placed on mobility. Even with some form of reciprocity, licensing nevertheless adds to the cost of movement.

Arlene S. Holen (1965) tested the effects of licensure on occupational mobility in medicine, dentistry, and law. She compared the ratios of members who moved to different states (from 1949 to 1950) with members who moved to different counties, both interstate and intrastate. Holen expected that the percentage of migrants who crossed state lines would be small when interstate mobility was restricted. Physicians were found to have the highest ratio (68 percent), while dentists and lawyers both were under 40 percent. This result is not surprising considering that reciprocity is usually more difficult to obtain in law and dentistry than in medicine.

Holen's findings were largely substantiated in 1980 studies by Bryan L. Boulier and Leila J. Pratt. Instead of formulating the

[1]*PRN*, November 1981, p. 3.
[2]Pashigian (1980, p. 301).

hypothesis in terms of income, Boulier used prices of services. He found that restricted mobility caused higher dental fees and lower output in some states than would otherwise be the case.

Using data from the same time period as Holen, Pratt broke down 16 occupations into 4 groups—occupations licensed by all states, by 30–49 states, by 1–29 states, and those that were not licensed. As expected, she found significant differences in mobility between groups. The greater the number of states licensing an occupation, the fewer "free" moves a practitioner had available, thus the more restricted his or her mobility.

A study by Morris M. Kleiner, Robert Gay, and Karen Greene provides more evidence on the impact of restrictive licensing laws on interstate mobility and earnings of professionals. For each state, an index was constructed to measure the relative restrictiveness of reciprocity provisions such that higher index numbers reflected greater restrictiveness. The model was based on 14 universally licensed occupations over the period 1965 to 1970. The results support the hypothesis that restrictive licensing may operate as a barrier to mobility and cause a misallocation of labor resources across states and increased earnings for practitioners. The authors explain:

> If our findings had shown that licensing restricts immigration but has no effect on earnings, then it could be assumed that the supply of instate practitioners is relatively inelastic. However, almost all of our estimates showed the effect of restrictive licensing was to increase the earnings of practitioners, which was economic rent to incumbents.[3]

Jeffrey M. Perloff's (1980) study of wages in construction trades refutes the notion that licensing laws cause a once-and-for-all wage increase when the law first goes into effect but no further effects. Because most jurisdictions that license construction trades have done so for decades, one might expect that the increase in construction wages brought on by licensure occurred years ago. However, licensing affects wage-rate changes to this day and was a major factor behind the spectacular rise of union wages between 1967 and 1974. Because licensing laws in the construction trades limit migration, the supply curve of labor becomes more inelastic than otherwise. In other words, wage rates could be high in certain jurisdic-

---

[3]Kleiner, Gay, and Greene (1982, p. 389).

tions, but licensing laws limit migration of workers into the more attractive areas.

The major implication of Perloff's study is that licensing, in addition to its initial effect, has been responsible for some of the large wage increases for construction workers by preventing wage equalization between construction and manufacturing. Eliminating the licensing restrictions would permit greater equalization of wages between these industries and thus increase efficiency.

As in the United States, the European Economic Community (EEC) is faced with the problem of reduced labor mobility caused by licensing restrictions. Each member nation of the EEC regulates professionals through licensing and other institutional arrangements. The EEC acknowledges the importance of allowing individual citizens in any member state to migrate and establish a practice in another country. Indeed, the benefits of "free factor mobility"—the unrestricted movement of capital and labor—served as a major justification for the establishment of the EEC. The details of specific requirements, however, differ from country to country, which results in long-standing conflicts over the coordination of national regulations. Unfortunately, resolving differences in occupational regulation is not a prime concern of the EEC. As a result, the EEC has a mixed record on breaking down migration barriers erected by licensing laws.[4]

---

[4]Orzack (1983, pp. 253–54).

# X. Licensing and Information Control

Professionals do not like to hear their "clients" described as "consumers" because the terms imply very different relationships between providers and receivers of service. Whereas clients deliver themselves into professional hands, consumers see themselves as buyers governed by caveat emptor.[1] Professionals count on an aura of mystery to surround the "truths" of their discipline. They present themselves to the public as the high priests of knowledge; they, and they alone, are privy to it. As Ivan Illich says, "Professionals tell you what you need. They claim the power to prescribe. They not only advertise what is good, but ordain what is right."[2]

Licensing laws promote consumer dependence on professional expertise; the implied philosophy of such laws is that consumers are incapable of properly evaluating information on practitioner competence. Only professionals are assumed to be in a position to judge performance. The implications of this control extend far beyond the market for professional services. "Inherent in the meaning of professionalism and the motives of its adherents," writes Jethro Lieberman, "is the negation of democracy itself, stemming from the incipient belief that the citizen, like the consumer, is incompetent to make important decisions affecting his life."[3]

The present wave of consumerism is a threat to such information control by professionals. The trend is manifest in various ways, from young professionals who recognize the value of client participation in determining how to solve client problems, to do-it-yourself books that reveal professional tricks-of-the-trade. Nowhere has this demystification become more apparent than in the legal profession.

In 1982 the U.S. Supreme Court ruled unanimously that lawyers' advertising may not be restricted by states except to protect con-

[1]Haug (1980, p. 75).
[2]Illich (1978, p. 342).
[3]Lieberman (1970, p. 7).

sumers from misleading advertisements. The decision reversed that of the Missouri Supreme Court, which had affirmed the state's restrictions on the style and content of attorneys' advertisements. This decision represents the High Court's strongest ruling regarding the rights of professionals to advertise. Justice Lewis Powell, who wrote the Court's opinion, noted that while states still have the legal right to regulate commercial speech that is inherently misleading, "the First and Fourteenth Amendments require that they do so with care and in a manner no more extensive than reasonably necessary."[4]

Partly because of the Supreme Court decision, legal clients are more inclined to view legal advice as simply another commodity one buys in the marketplace, much like television sets or automobiles. Any person with at least a high school education who is willing to spend some time with a legal reference book written for the layman soon realizes that most of the work performed by lawyers is fairly routine and repetitive, not the glamorous, intellectually demanding work associated with famous trial cases. Few consumers need a first-rate trial lawyer; their needs are much more mundane. They usually require no more than an expert who knows what forms to fill out, how to fill them out, and where to file them. Much to the dismay of mainstream attorneys, an ever-increasing number of consumers, in their newfound knowledge and confidence, are entering into arrangements with lawyers not as helpless children desperately in need of paternal guidance but as equals in a voluntary exchange. Advertising, especially by low-cost legal clinics, has advanced this trend even further by informing consumers that indeed they do have options in the purchase of legal services.

Nevertheless, many professional codes of ethics outside the legal profession still constrain advertising, limit brand-name identification, and discourage public evaluation of professionals' work. At first appearance, these forms of information control may seem to conflict with assertions that the market for professional services is marked by information asymmetry and thus requires a regulatory response. After all, advertising, brand names, and public evaluations of professional performance mitigate the asymmetry problem

[4]*PRN*, January 1982, p. 1.

by conveying important information to consumers. Without advertising and other forms of competitive activity, consumers must produce their own information from sources, such as word of mouth, that are imperfect substitutes for the constant flow of information that competitive activity provides. In the absence of such activity, consumer choices are poorer and consumer welfare is less than it could be.

In fact, however, information control and the asymmetry argument represent the same philosophy: the assumption that most individuals are incapable of coping with a commercial environment. The asymmetry argument is based on the notion that in the absence of licensing laws an unregulated market would generate inadequate service quality. Information control is defended on the grounds that liars, cheats, and incompetents would use information channels to deceive consumers or create artificial wants. The implication is that competition, while beneficial when applied to producers in general, needs to be severely constrained when applied to the professions.

Unfettered competition, it is argued, will destroy the competitive process through cutthroat pricing, which drives out competitors, leaving the market to a few dominant survivors who can then gouge consumers. The notion of destructive competition was the dominant rationale for much of the economic regulation of the New Deal. Airlines and trucking are prominent examples of industries in which extensive government control of prices and production was introduced because competition was thought to be the cause of severe economic problems. (Both industries are now deregulated to a large extent.)

Forty years of history and economic research, however, have taught us that depressions are not caused by the competitive structure of individual markets. A case in which destructive competition could be documented as a cause of poor performance in an industry has rarely been observed.[5] In fact, not only was the regulation created in the 1930s ineffective in coping with the Great Depression, it led to inefficiencies when recovery did take place. Nevertheless, the destructive-competition argument is often invoked in regulatory proceedings and used by professional groups to argue for competitive restraints.

---

[5]Noll and Owen (1983, p. 54).

As expected, the major effects of information control are reduced competition and higher prices, not consumer protection. The most dramatic evidence on this point is Lee Benham's 1972 study on the effects of advertising restrictions on the price of eyeglasses. Benham found that states that prohibited advertising (controlling for other factors) had prices that were 25 to 40 percent higher than other states. In addition, he found that eyeglasses have a price elasticity of $-1.0$, which means that prices which are 25 to 40 percent *higher* correspond to a 25 to 40 percent *decline* in the quantity demanded. The eyecare of affluent consumers—for whom eyeglasses are relatively price inelastic—is unlikely to be affected by higher prices. A difference in price between, say, $75 and $100 is unlikely to be decisive. Low-income consumers, on the other hand, are more likely to be on the margin. Higher prices translate into lower demand, resulting in suboptimal eyecare. Indeed, optometrists have claimed that use of eyecare services in the United States is only half of the optimal rate.[6]

A 1984 FTC report based on a survey of 3,200 lawyers in 17 states found that fees for ordinary legal services—simple wills, simple wills with a trust provision, nonbusiness bankruptcies, uncontested divorces, and personal injury cases—were 5 to 13 percent lower in states with relatively few restrictions on advertising.[7] For example, the price for handling a personal bankruptcy in a restrictive state was $44 above the average of $460. The study also found that prices decline as advertising increases in legal services markets, and that lawyers who advertise a specific service tend to provide it at a lower price than lawyers who do not advertise. Moreover, the FTC found no indication that advertising leads to a deterioration in the quality of legal services.

Although the benefits of price advertising in medicine may be less apparent than in law, an attorney with the FTC's Bureau of Competition claims:

> The disinclination of individual physicians to advertise will gradually decrease as insurers continue to increase the size of deductibles that patients must pay out-of-pocket; as physicians perceive an excess supply of competitors in their communities; and as

---

[6]Benham and Benham (1975, p. 446).
[7]Federal Trade Commission (1984).

> physicians experience increased competitive pressures from nonphysician health care providers. . . . It does not take many newspaper ads announcing primary care physician fees to raise a question in the minds of readers as to whether the fees of their family physicians who do not advertise are in the same ball park.[8]

The American College of Physicians disagrees with this view, of course, calling the FTC's approach to professional advertising "cold-blooded" and a threat to the intimacy of the physician/patient relationship. However, as the FTC's former chairman James C. Miller III says of organized medicine's anticompetitive practices,

> These activities have little or nothing to do with the quality of medical care that's offered. They're commercial activities, good old-fashioned business practices that happen to violate the antitrust laws. I don't think they should be overlooked simply because individuals with advanced degrees are engaging in them.[9]

Some professional groups are especially disturbed by the FTC's recent efforts to expand its intervention beyond price advertising. The commission now recognizes that advertising does more than simply apply downward pressure on prices; it promotes a substantial restructuring of the marketplace by encouraging specialization and the development of more efficient systems for delivering professional services (for instance, legal clinics and prepaid health plans).[10]

Since the Supreme Court's 1982 ruling on legal advertising, the dental profession has been cautiously trying to draw a fine line between false advertising and the merely flamboyant. The ruling prohibited broad-based advertising restrictions, but nonetheless, dentists have tried to impose controls on maverick advertisers. The Texas Board of Dental Examiners in 1984 disciplined a dentist who promoted his clinics with a money-back guarantee, discount coupons, a 12-foot tooth, and the motto, "We cater to cowards." Other states have expressed concern over advertisements that imply specialization. The Missouri Dental Association, for example, requested the state dental board to investigate use of such terms as "family

---

[8]*PRN*, October/November 1985, pp. 3–4.
[9]Warner (1982).
[10]*PRN*, October/November 1985, p. 4.

practice," "cosmetic dentistry," and "children's dentistry" in Yellow Pages and newspaper ads.[11] An Illinois rule that forbids an advertisement to imply a specialty was upheld in federal district court. Phrases such as "cosmetic dentistry" may be used but only if they include disclaimers indicating that the specialty is not recognized by the state.[12]

The amount of information made available to consumers strikes at the heart of the information-control controversy. In medicine, for example, how much information do patients want and deserve regarding their own health and treatment? A benevolent paternalism still prevails among physicians who believe patients would rather leave decisions to them. A study by the Rand Corporation, however, casts doubt on this belief. The study found that 70 percent of first-time users of drugs read the instructions and warning inserts accompanying the drugs. Half keep them for reference and about a quarter read them more than once.[13] Pharmacists and physicians have been opposed to these little flyers because they interfere with the doctor/patient relationship. Not surprisingly, the American Society of Internal Medicine criticized the Rand study for faulty design and stated its belief that inserts have little influence on actual patient behavior.

If there is an overall trend on such issues, it seems to be in the direction of fewer restrictions. Many courts are ruling out limitations on the type of media used for advertisements. For example, an Illinois law limiting dental ads to general circulation newspapers in a dentist's own community recently was struck down by a federal judge who said it went much farther than necessary to prevent potential deception.

In summary, about the best that can be said for restrictions on advertising, competitive bidding, and solicitation is that their connection with quality is tenuous. There is no warrant for assuming that advertising and other competitive behavior lead to lower overall quality in the professions any more than in other markets. Even

---

[11]Examples are from *PRN*, July 1984, p. 4.
[12]*PRN*, October 1985, p. 7.
[13]*PRN*, September 1981, p. 7.

if average quality were reduced by advertising, the substantially lower prices that often result could be more consistent with consumer preferences than the current quality/price trade-offs mandated by law—especially for low-income consumers.

# XI. Licensing and Innovation

> Had retailing been organized like the professions, supermarkets with lower costs and prices and a wider range of goods and services could never have emerged. Indeed, had the professions been dominant through manufacture and trade over the past two centuries, we would never have got to the horse-and-buggy stage, let alone beyond it.
>
> —D. S. Lees[1]

Licensing laws have exerted a negative influence in many professions by inhibiting innovations in practice, training, education, and organization of services. The most prominent examples in recent years are the efforts of the organized medical profession to inhibit prepaid health plans and of lawyers to ban low-cost legal clinics.

The most effective way of inhibiting innovation in licensed professions is through disciplinary provisions of the laws. The American Medical Association's (AMA) fight against prepaid group health plans is a case in point. The AMA has the power to approve intern and residency programs in hospitals. Medical licensing laws generally require a candidate to complete an internship in an "approved" hospital before being admitted to practice, and often a licensing board's list of approved hospitals is identical to the AMA list. The AMA has used this threat of disapproval to coerce hospitals into denying access to physicians affiliated with prepaid plans. AMA disapproval can cause severe financial hardship to a hospital, because it then has difficulty obtaining interns and residents to help operate the hospital.[2]

Despite setbacks in a series of antitrust suits, the AMA continues its opposition to nontraditional forms of medical service. According to the medical establishment, the new health care delivery systems emphasize cost cutting at the expense of sound clinical judgment.

---

[1] Lees (1966, p. 28).
[2] Rayack (1983, p. 151).

There is little doubt, however, that organized medicine's stand is motivated primarily by economic factors. Physicians fear losing patients to the plans. Moreover, under prepaid plans, physicians lack the control over income that is possible under a fee-for-service system. By using its licensing and accreditation powers to restrain innovations that could improve the quality or reduce the cost of medical care, organized medicine harms consumers.[3] Ironically, the growth of prepaid plans has created a countergroup of health care professionals with vested interests in preserving and expanding this form of health care delivery. Their influence, combined with the near-universal recognition that these programs make good economic sense, ensures that prepaid health plans are here to stay.

The health plan controversy in medicine is closely paralleled by the battle over low-cost legal clinics. Prepaid group practice makes considerable sense in the legal profession, because many attorneys spend much of their time and earn most of their income doing relatively simple paperwork. Thus, much legal work is amenable to high-volume, low-cost group practice. Just as the corner grocer has been crowded out by supermarkets offering greater variety at lower prices, so the one-man law firm is on the way out. Mainstream lawyers, of course, find this turn of events distressing. Not only do legal clinics take business away from them, but the law is being transformed "from priestly knowledge to a mere commodity bought in the marketplace."[4]

Professionals also are resistant to innovative forms of practice ownership. This fact has become apparent in the ongoing debate over whether nonprofessionals should be permitted to obtain ownership interests in professional firms.[5] A strong argument exists for such an approach. Providing professional service requires a different set of skills from marketing such service. Indeed, many high-quality professionals are not good salesmen. Optimal market service for such professionals might be achieved by selling ownership interests to entrepreneurs with special marketing skills. So long as tort law, rigorous enforcement of ethics codes, and ordinary market incentives hold professionals to high standards for their output,

[3]Ibid.
[4]Greene (1984, p. 76).
[5]Beales (1980, p. 139).

nonprofessional ownership should not present a serious quality-control problem.

Professional groups insist, however, that entrepreneurs, unlike their members, are motivated mainly by profits rather than peer approval. Therefore, if professionals are hired by nonprofessional entrepreneurs, professional control will be weakened. To illustrate, the California Optometric Association successfully lobbied against legislation that would have lifted certain restrictions on corporate ownership of optometry services. In January 1984, as a response to the threat posed by such legislation, the association asked the Federal Trade Commission to launch a full-scale investigation of franchised optometric centers. The association's president said in a news conference:

> We have issued this formal request because we are gravely concerned with the impact that this legislation will have on the quality of vision care in California. . . . The consuming public would be jeopardized if a large manufacturer or corporation with pecuniary profits as its principal goal or motive were allowed to control the professional judgment or decision rendered by the medical profession.[6]

Of course, professional groups have favored changing forms of ownership when their economic interests will be served. The practice of medicine by corporations, for example, was outlawed until federal tax advantages of corporate practice altered the economic equation. Physicians lobbied legislatures to change the laws just enough to permit use of the tax advantages without permitting threatening new forms of practice to emerge.[7]

Licensing can hinder innovation in more subtle ways. In the medical profession, for example, the nature of licensing exams, the areas in which an examinee is tested, and the requirement that an applicant graduate from an AMA-approved medical school ensure that medical education is highly standardized. Yet there is little evidence that current programs and teaching methods are superior to alternatives.[8] One critic writes:

---

[6]*PRN*, February 1984, pp. 2–3.
[7]Dolan (1980, p. 37).
[8]Hogan (1979, p. 280).

> Because the educational pathways to entry tend to be monolithic due to strict accreditation devices, the graduates of professional training reflect a uniformity of professional and therapeutic ideology which reduces the diversity of services available to consumers. This in turn discourages and often forbids any experimentation in the training sector with new and more cost-effective educational methods.[9]

In many fields advances have resulted from the very crackpots, quacks, and outsiders with no standing in the profession that licensure seeks to eliminate. For example, Thomas Edison had little formal education and thus, under modern guidelines, could not be a licensed engineer. Likewise, Mies van der Rohe and Frank Lloyd Wright would not qualify to sit for the architect's certifying examination under the current education requirement. If registered dieticians in Illinois succeed in prohibiting nonlicensees from providing nutrition and diet information, innovative nutrition pioneers like Nathan Pritikin will be barred from practicing in the state.[10] The leaders in the fight to establish inoculation as a cure for smallpox in colonial America were Cotton Mather and his fellow clergymen; their leading opponents were doctors.[11] As Milton Friedman writes,

> There are many different routes to knowledge and learning and the effect of restricting the practice of what is called medicine and confining it . . . to a particular group, who in the main have to conform to the prevailing orthodoxy, is certain to reduce the amount of experimentation that goes on and hence to reduce the rate of growth and knowledge in the area.[12]

---

[9]Dolan (1980, p. 36).
[10]Lynn (1986, pp. 1–2).
[11]Lieberman (1970, p. 10).
[12]Friedman (1962, p. 157).

## XII. Effects on Minorities and the Poor

> There are many laws in the United States that discriminate against the employment and advancement of people who are outsiders, latecomers, and poor in resources. It is important to point out that these laws or rules discriminate against certain people irrespective of race. However, because of their history in the U.S., blacks are disproportionately represented in the class of people described as outsiders, latecomers, and resourceless.
>
> —Walter Williams[1]

Even the harshest critics of licensing would not argue that occupational regulation is purposefully discriminatory by race, but any regulation that imposes barriers to entry is likely to have adverse effects on outsiders who want to become insiders. One problem with licensing laws is that in our society, minorities are more likely to be outsiders than insiders.

While licensing statutes are no longer deliberately biased, this was not always the case. After Reconstruction and before the civil rights movement of the 1960s, state governments in the South were run almost exclusively for the benefit of white citizens. Not surprisingly, policies were designed to redistribute income and opportunities in favor of whites and against blacks. This era was also marked by a dramatic increase in the number of licensed occupations in the United States and the number of states that licensed them. Licensing boards that sprang up in the South during this period always came under white domination. By setting formal education requirements that few blacks could meet, and by imposing discriminatory application procedures, these boards substantially reduced competition from black craftsmen and thus raised the wages of white workers.

Racial discrimination also extended to the learned professions, of course, although the instrument for promoting bias was not always

---

[1]Williams (1982, p. xvi).

in the form of a licensing law. For example, until the late 1960s, many local medical societies in the South denied membership to black doctors. Although membership in state societies was not required for licensure, a physician's ability to conduct a practice was greatly restricted without it. Without local society membership, doctors were effectively barred from participation in scientific programs, specialty board ratings, referrals and consultations, and affiliation with most hospitals. Legal efforts to enjoin medical societies from barring black physicians were unsuccessful because of the widely accepted belief that such societies were private, fraternal organizations and therefore not obligated to give equal protection to blacks.[2]

Abraham Flexner's famous 1910 study of medical education in the United States, known as the Flexner Report, also had an adverse effect on the upward mobility of blacks. The report persuaded state legislators throughout the country to limit licensure to graduates of medical schools approved (expressly or implicitly) by the AMA. The result was the large-scale closing of schools unable to meet the AMA's high standards. The number of medical schools in the United States declined from 131 in 1910 to 85 in 1920, 76 in 1930, and 69 in 1944.[3]

Some of the medical schools that closed specialized in training black doctors. In the early years of the 20th century, the percentage of black doctors increased sharply, but with the decline in the number of black medical schools from seven in 1910 to two in 1944, this percentage leveled off at its 1910 peak.[4]

In the blue-collar trades, white-controlled labor unions were among the most vociferous and avid supporters of licensure. Plumbers, electricians, and railroad firemen all lobbied for licensing laws with the express purpose of excluding blacks. In some states, union efforts were so successful that blacks were eliminated from practicing a given craft. When markets were allowed to work, blacks apparently had relatively little difficulty competing with whites for jobs, but licensing laws and restrictive trade union practices resulted in the systematic exclusion of blacks from the skilled trades. Of

---

[2]Lieberman (1970, pp. 25–27).
[3]Kessel (1958, p. 28).
[4]Kessel (1970, p. 270).

course, discrimination was also practiced in the North but not nearly on the scale of the South.

Richard Freeman (1980) provides evidence on this point. He examined 17 trades in 7 southern states between 1890 and 1960; for comparative purposes, similar information was gathered on 4 nonsouthern states. He found that licensing laws in the South significantly reduced the penetration of blacks into the crafts, while such laws in the nonsouthern states had little or no impact. For the southern states, the relative penetration of blacks—that is, the fraction of workers in a given craft who were black divided by the fraction of all workers in the state who were black—was 33 percent lower in licensed crafts than in nonlicensed crafts. By comparison, relative penetration for the nonsouthern states was only 4 percent lower for the licensed crafts.

Although Freeman found that by 1970 licensure no longer seemed to be a major barrier to black advancement, other evidence indicates that licensure may adversely affect black workers even today. Stuart Dorsey considered the effects on workers of exclusion from an occupation by failure of a licensing examination. Licensing exams often contain two parts—written and practical. The potential for bias may be greater on the written test because candidates with poor reading ability or whose first language is not English are often at a disadvantage. Moreover, better-educated candidates usually have more experience with testing in general, which increases their chances for success on written tests. Trade school graduates also have an advantage over those licensing candidates who acquire their training through apprenticeships. Indeed, it is typical for licensing exams to parallel the course work in trade schools, and vice versa, which is hardly surprising given that the success of private trade schools depends largely on the success of their graduates in obtaining licenses.

Dorsey's test involved applicants for beautician licenses in Missouri and Illinois. He found that each year of general education raised the chances of passing by 2.9 percent for Missouri and 2.1 percent for Illinois applicants. Blacks in Missouri had a pass rate that was 30 percent lower than whites, even with education and training held constant. Similar results were found for Illinois applicants. Those who received their basic education outside the United States, or who received their occupational training by apprenticeship, also had markedly lower pass rates, with all other variables held constant.

When scores from the practical examination were considered, however, the results were very different. Whereas general education, race, apprenticing, and foreign school training all had significant effects on pass rates of the written exam, only race had a significant effect on passage of the practical exam. Moreover, the effect of race was quite small relative to its effect on scores on the written exam. These results led Dorsey to conclude:

> The written examination excludes workers on the basis of characteristics that, with the possible exception of race, are unrelated to ability as evaluated by the practical examination. . . . Written licensing examinations for [beautician] licenses appear to be biased against the less educated, apprentices, blacks, and nonnatives. The implication is that the losses suffered by rejected applicants . . . will be concentrated among these groups.[5]

Licensing raises entry costs, thereby causing some potential entrants to decide against pursuing the occupation. No one is explicitly rejected; people decide not to try in the first place.[6] The consequences of the bias described by Dorsey can include unemployment, choosing less desirable occupations, and practicing without a license. The third option is particularly common in the inner cities, where enforcement of licensing regulations is often weak. In his discussions with inner-city residents in St. Louis and Chicago, Dorsey found that beauticians and barbers routinely circumvented the law and provided service in their homes.[7]

The widespread existence of unlicensed tradesmen in the inner cities points out another problem with licensing laws from the viewpoint of the poor. Although licensing may reduce the number of poorly qualified or unqualified practitioners in a given trade or profession, it also raises costs to consumers. Licensing schemes, by conveying a quality signal, can serve to reduce uncertainty for consumers, but less uncertainty can be had only for a price, and that price may be too high for some consumers. Those consumers prefer to assume more risk in exchange for lower prices. As D. S.

---

[5]Dorsey (1980, p. 433).
[6]Williams (1982, p. 71).
[7]Dorsey (1983).

Lees states, "Professional insistence on high minimum standards is technological, not economic. It treats some given reduction of uncertainty as desirable in itself and not, as it correctly should, as simply another choice that consumers make in their complex of choices."[8]

The case mentioned previously of Illinois's registered dieticians (RDs) promoting legislation that would give them control over all nutrition and diet information in the state is illustrative. People seeking nutritional advice would be required to consult with a physician before seeing an RD, meaning that a patient would have to pay twice: once for a doctor and once for an RD. A report of the Heartland Institute in Chicago charges that the increased cost of nutritional advice that would likely result from this legislation would be most harmful to those who need such advice the most—the poor and the elderly. "Priced out of the market," the report says, "these people will no longer have ready access to a form of health care that is safer and less disruptive of families and careers than the conventional treatments by medication or surgery."[9]

Even though some consumers may be willing to pay for a level of quality below that which is mandated by law, the option is simply not available. The result is a "Cadillac effect," in which consumers either purchase the services of high-quality practitioners at a high price or purchase no services at all. Unlicensed practitioners in the inner city may not meet the quality standards imposed by law, but they provide service at prices their constituents can afford. (This justification does not imply a demand for incompetent heart surgeons—a common straw-man argument of licensure advocates—but recognizes a potentially large market for low-quality professional service in many of the tasks now reserved for licensed practitioners, from accountancy to legal work.) If markets are to become price competitive, some sellers must be willing, as one writer puts it, "to deviate from 'nice' cooperative behavior and cut their prices. . . . Price cutters tend to be the fringe producers, those who differ from the cartel-establishment in background, interests, and pedigree."[10]

---

[8]Lees (1966, p. 13).
[9]Lynn (1986, p. 2).
[10]Pauly (1985).

Sidney Carroll and Robert Gaston in 1981 examined the relationship between restrictiveness in the licensing requirements for electricians and accidental deaths by electric shock. In a startling confirmation of the Cadillac effect, they found that restrictions, by reducing the number of journeyman electricians and raising costs to consumers, were significantly associated with rates of electrocution. Consumers did their own electrical work rather than pay artificially high rates for professionals, with predictably tragic results. Carroll and Gaston also found that plumbing restrictions increased the extent of do-it-yourself work as measured by retail sales of plumbing equipment.

Another noteworthy example of the Cadillac effect concerns the well-publicized case of a Florida woman, Rosemary Furman, who provides a low-cost legal-forms service to the poor. She was recently sentenced to 30 days in jail for practicing law without a license, despite the absence of evidence suggesting lack of accountability or competence. However, a feature segment on the popular "60 Minutes" television program and nationwide press coverage induced Florida's governor to issue a clemency order, thus allowing Furman to avoid jail.

# XIII. Professionals and the Scope of Practice

Litigation such as that surrounding the Rosemary Furman case stems in part from the tendency of all professions to define as broadly as possible what practice is restricted to licensees. Licensing laws are often called "practice acts," because they grant authority to licensees to engage in certain practices within a profession. Once the scope of practice is established by law, it is illegal for anyone without a license to perform any of the activities covered by the law. Professionals guard their turf jealously and will even attempt to broaden the scope of what is restricted.

Lawyers are especially notorious guardians. Years ago, they fought accountants over the right to give tax advice, with the legal profession predictably arguing that such service constitutes the practice of law. More recently, several bar associations have sought to prevent real estate brokers and others from performing simple, routine tasks that lawyers allege to be legal work.

Turf disputes are particularly common in the market for health care services. To illustrate, in 1984 state officials in New York warned pedicurists not to cut corns, calluses, and ingrown toenails because such services were deemed to constitute the practice of podiatry without a license. Understandably, the Podiatry Society of the State of New York applauded the action, calling it a fine example of cooperation between government and professional societies.[1]

The often brazen protectionism of licensure prompted sociologist Marie Haug to write:

> Licensing arrangements . . . can be characterized less as methods for protecting the public and for providing external social control in the interest of the consumer than as a means for protecting the occupation's market dominance. Indeed, licensing has the unique

---

[1]*PRN*, December 1984, pp. 6–7.

quality of making a violation of the professional monopoly a punishable crime.[2]

This protectionism has come under attack in recent years. Concern over escalating costs in medicine, dentistry, and other professions has generated considerable interest in the use of paraprofessionals to help bring down costs. The scope of practice as defined by some licensing laws, however, severely constrains the activities of paraprofessionals, even though they may be qualified to perform many of the activities commonly reserved for professionals.

A Canadian government survey of dental practice showed that as much as 80 to 90 percent of the work performed by general dentists can be performed by a high school graduate with only 20 months of post–secondary-school training. Another study estimates that dental care costs in Ontario could be reduced by as much as 40 percent if dentists were to make optimal use of paraprofessionals.[3]

Similar results have been found in the medical profession in this country. A 1984 study by the Senate Select Committee on Aging recommended greater use of nurse practitioners and physicians' assistants to perform procedures not requiring a physician's expertise. Based on a year-long study of health care for the elderly in other countries, the report called on the United States to "follow the lead of those nations that have been able to improve the balance of values in care provided through the upgrading and increased utilization of nurses."[4] The report notes that when health care administrators try to cut costs, access to care is usually cut in favor of preserving quality. For a better balance, the committee urges more use of nonphysicians.

According to a survey conducted by the National Center for Health Statistics, in 1980 more than one-third of the American people visited a health practitioner other than a physician or dentist to obtain health services. One in 8 U.S. residents visited a nurse at least once during the year, one in 11 visited an optometrist, one in 15 a laboratory technician, one in 25 a chiropractor, one in 37 a radiological technician, one in 50 a podiatrist, and one in 100 a

[2]Haug (1980, p. 67).
[3]Evans (1980, p. 242).
[4]*PRN*, April/May 1984, p. 6.

paramedic, physical therapist, or psychologist.[5] (The visits were counted only if they were made independently of a visit to a physician or dentist, or if they occurred in a hospital emergency room or while the person was a hospital inpatient.)

Few professions make adequate use of paraprofessionals. Practitioners often claim that paraprofessionals are less efficient than fully trained professionals and thus less likely to be accepted by consumers. Yet empirical research indicates that auxiliaries are quickly accepted by consumers who have dealt with them.[6]

Ironically, considerable progress on this issue has been made in the home of regulation, Washington, D.C. The City Council enacted the Health Care Facility and Licensure Act of 1983 to prohibit class discrimination against five groups of health care providers—podiatrists, psychologists, nurse practitioners, nurse anesthetists, and nurse midwives—in the granting of clinical privileges.[7] The most far-reaching measure of its kind, the bill requires hospitals to evaluate an applicant's credentials on an individual basis. Reasonable, nondiscriminatory standards must be applied, and evaluation must be free of anticompetitive intent. Membership in a professional society, advertising practices, charges for services, or collaboration with other classes of health professions are all prohibited from consideration in the evaluation process. What makes this legislation unique is its comprehensiveness. Many states have given protection to nonphysicians, but in an ad hoc fashion rather than through extending clinical privileges to several groups at once.

Progress also has been made elsewhere. As a result of a 1984 ballot referendum, Montana became the third state to permit denturists to make, fit, and repair removable dentalwork without referral from a dentist.[8] The Montana Dental Association opposed the initiative, charging that denturists cannot be relied on to recognize injured or diseased tissues.

In 1986 Colorado became the first state to pass a law permitting dental hygienists to open independent dental hygiene clinics. A key factor cited in winning legislative approval for the new law was

---

[5]National Center for Health Statistics (1984).
[6]Hogan (1979, p. 277).
[7]*PRN*, October 1983, p. 5.
[8]*PRN*, December 1984, p. 5.

the state's seven years of experience in allowing hygienists to practice unsupervised in nursing homes, public schools, and other institutions. During that time, no complaints were made against hygienists practicing in those settings. The director of Colorado's Department of Regulatory Agencies claimed that the measure "begins a new era in the provision of dental care in the United States. . . . [The bill] shows that we will aggressively fight against special interest abuse of the regulatory process."[9]

The case of nurse-midwives in Massachusetts provides a good example of what can happen when professionals feel threatened by encroachment and what others can do to retaliate. In 1981 the state legislature voted to override Governor Edward J. King's veto of a bill that permitted nurse-midwives to perform deliveries in independent birth centers not connected with hospitals. Nurse-midwives and their supporters were confident of the governor's support as late as the day he vetoed the bill. Suspicions thus arose as to why the governor changed his mind so late. Said one supporter, "We got hold of the letter the medical society wrote to King after the bill passed, and it was almost word for word what he said in his veto. We used that to the fullest."[10] Legislators were angry at the protectionist attitude of the medical society and retaliated by overriding the veto. In addition, many legislators were swayed by the enormous cost savings afforded by the bill. A pilot project using midwives found that services costing $2,200 in a hospital cost only $800 in the birthing center. The center also had a good safety record.

Restrictions on the scope of activities delegated to paraprofessionals can be especially damaging to minorities and the poor who are much more likely to attain paraprofessional status than to become fully trained professionals. Restrictions reduce their employment opportunities and thus important opportunities for upward mobility. In addition, inadequate use of professional auxiliaries unnecessarily raises costs to consumers, which not only imposes hardship on low-income consumers who pay for services but also reduces their chances of seeking and receiving adequate care in the first place.

Another effect of broad and overly vague definitions of profes-

[9]*PRN*, March 1986, p. 5.
[10]*PRN*, February 1982, p. 1.

sional practice is to foster maldistribution in the supply of services in certain geographical areas. Stringent supervisory requirements regarding paraprofessionals contribute to this problem.[11] In rural areas, for example, effective use of midwives is prevented by "over-the-shoulder" and "on-the-premises" supervision requirements. When taken to extremes, reluctance to delegate routine tasks to nonprofessionals can be nonsensical. To illustrate, a local medical society in California brought charges of practicing medicine without a license against a surgeon's assistant who, under instructions, removed stitches from a patient's incision.[12]

---

[11]Hogan (1983, p. 127).
[12]Trombetta (1982, p. 109).

# XIV. The Reform Movement and the Future

> In an advanced society, important inequalities of knowledge and technical understanding multiply. Every citizen is incompetent in many areas. . . . It does not follow that rule by experts is an intelligent response to the new inequalities. It is still wise to trust the ordinary wisdom of plain human beings on juries, in the voting booth, in the development of public dialogue, and in the ordinary decencies of daily living. So also, it would seem, a wise society trusts individuals to spend their hard-earned dollars as they judge best.
>
> —Michael Novak[1]

Reforms of state licensing boards have been implemented in many states by adding so-called public representatives to the boards, the use of umbrella agencies to supervise professional boards in the state, and the passage of sunset and sunrise laws. Despite some noteworthy achievements, however, the reform movement's efforts to improve the public accountability of licensing boards have been disappointing. Ironically, the most successful reform efforts have come from the federal government, in the form of rulings by the Federal Trade Commission (FTC).

## Public Members

The failure of public members to reform regulatory boards has been caused by several factors. First, inclusion of the lay public on boards has met with considerable resistance from practitioners who perceive the board as a mechanism for upholding standards—a task they feel is best left to professionals. In their view, professionals keep a watchful eye on their peers; the layman does not have a useful role to play. Public accountability, on the other hand, implies that laymen, in addition to professionals, should judge competence

---

[1]Novak (1982, p. 107).

and integrity. This idea runs counter to the claim that professional expertise is so rarefied and unique that only those trained in it should be allowed to judge performance.

Second, the role of the public member is inadequately defined.[2] Little thought has been given to what the public member should do on the board or what qualifications should be required for appointment. In some states the only requirement is a willingness to attend board meetings. The result is a tendency to fill public-member vacancies by the patronage system, with appointments going to those who worked in the governor's campaign or made sizable financial contributions.

Third, advocates of the public-member concept do not understand the psychological and economic strains under which public members operate. Benjamin Shimberg's 1982 study provides several examples:

- Professional members often derive prestige within their peer group from serving on a board, but the public member does not. For the layman, it may be a thankless job.
- Professional members are likely to be very interested in professional issues, but public members' primary interests lie elsewhere.
- Professional members usually are willing to devote substantial time to board activities, because these are viewed as an extension of their professional lives. Because public members' stakes in licensing are small, they may be unwilling to devote much time to the board if it takes them away from their regular jobs.
- Professional members usually are familiar with licensing procedures. Public members are much less likely to be familiar with such matters.
- Professional members can draw from the resources of professional associations in order to keep informed about emerging issues. Public members have no comparable source of assistance to which they can turn.

### Umbrella Agencies

The results of umbrella, or central, oversight agencies are not much better. The idea here is to centralize administration of licens-

---

[2]Shimberg (1982, p. 165).

ing laws and thus deprive occupational groups of direct regulatory control. Grouping autonomous boards into a single central agency does not mean, however, that autonomy of the individual boards has been curbed in any significant way.[3] Typically, boards have been centralized in the interest of promoting greater efficiency in administration, not to promote deregulation or greater public accountability. The central agency may be responsible for general housekeeping activities (such as answering phones, processing license renewals, and other routine chores) and may indeed be successful in this function. For example, centralization efforts in New Mexico improved record-keeping, accounting, and office location.[4] Before consolidation, board offices were scattered throughout the state and relocated whenever a new chairman was elected. All board offices are now located on one floor of a building in Santa Fe.

In most states, however, the boards, not the umbrella agencies, retain autonomy over the most crucial aspects of licensing—approving applications, setting standards for practice and conduct, preparing and grading exams, and disciplining licensees. They usually control their own budgets and hire their own staff. A few states do have central agencies that exercise significantly more control than housekeeping, but for the most part, umbrella arrangements have done little to improve accountability.

**Sunset Laws**

Sunset legislation is another response to the perceived need for more accountability in the administration of regulatory bodies. Such legislation requires that regulatory laws, agencies, or programs be terminated at a specific date unless re-created by the state legislature. The hope is that legislators will be forced to evaluate the results of regulations.

Since 1976 when Colorado passed the first sunset law, more than 30 states have enacted such legislation. Between 1976 and 1982, 1,500 agencies nationwide were reviewed under the sunset process. About one in five were terminated, one in three were modified, and somewhat less than half were left virtually or completely intact.[5]

---

[3]Ibid., p. 26.
[4]*PRN*, February 1986, p. 5.
[5]*PRN*, March 1982, p. 2.

While the numbers may seem impressive, little progress has been made at eliminating or reforming state licensing boards, even though these boards have been especially popular targets of sunset-law movements. Alaska's legislature placed 21 boards under review in 1981, for example, but only the collection-agency board was dissolved.[6] Michigan brought an end to its 15-year-old horology (watchmaking) board, thus letting the licenses of the state's 527 horologists expire. Even in this rather trivial case, however, opposition was strong enough that the termination provision had to be pushed through the legislature as a rider on an unrelated bill.[7]

A South Carolina official charges that, although legislators are enthusiastic about approving sunset legislation, their enthusiasm wanes when specific boards are in question. A sunset law was passed in South Carolina without dissent, but when the state's reorganization commission recommended a minor change—the merger of the barber and cosmetology boards—the proposal was overwhelmingly defeated in the state legislature.[8] A Common Cause survey of state government officials throughout the country confirms that pressure from professional associations is the major reason legislators are inclined to vote against sunset review recommendations to deregulate.

Charles Robb encountered a similar problem when, as governor of Virginia, he promoted a program that would have deregulated several occupations in the state. Since Virginia is more committed than most states to free enterprise and limited government, Robb's reform drive was generally well received. But as one observer noted, "Deregulation in theory is universally praised, while deregulation in practice means eternal struggle with businesses and professions that benefit from regulation."[9]

This truth became apparent when beauticians in Virginia challenged proposed reforms that would have subjected them to competition from "unqualified" hairdressers. State officials were bombarded with letters of protest, and petitions were circulated in beauty salons throughout the state. The hairdressers' lobbyist accused

---

[6]*PRN*, October 1981, p. 3.
[7]*PRN*, August 1981, p. 6.
[8]*PRN*, October 1981, p. 3.
[9]Isikoff (1983).

the author of the proposal, the director of Virginia's Board of Commerce, of threatening "the aesthetic welfare of the ladies of the commonwealth." Another critic argued that the new policy would lead to an upsurge in female baldness.[10]

A Colorado state representative aptly described the problem for legislators:

> Most legislators don't enjoy sunset because they haven't figured out how to make it pay off. It does two things to legislators: it takes a lot of time and it gets them into trouble with their constituency over things they don't need to get in trouble with.[11]

Recent developments in sunset laws are not encouraging. Some states abolished the concept after program evaluations went through the first cycle of legislative review. Also, the number of regulatory boards subject to review has declined, and the review cycle has been lengthened in many cases (for example, the typical six-year cycle has been increased to eight or ten years).[12]

**Sunrise Laws**

Minnesota recently became the first state to implement a sunrise program, which requires that occupations satisfy several criteria before licensing is instituted. The factors considered by the state's advisory council include the potential for public harm from unregulated practice, whether specialized skills or training are required, whether effective public protection exists through nonregulatory means, and the overall cost-effectiveness and economic impact of the proposed regulation.[13] If the application for regulation is denied, the occupational group must wait two years before refiling. Michigan has begun a similar program.

**The Federal Government and Reform**

Although most government involvement in the professions occurs at the state level, the federal government (in particular, the FTC) has expanded its role in recent years. Under the chairmanship of

---

[10]Ibid.
[11]*PRN*, September/October 1984, p. 9.
[12]Ibid., pp. 9–10.
[13]Ibid., p. 10; *PRN* January 1986, pp. 2–3.

James C. Miller III (now head of the Office of Management and Budget), the FTC adopted an activist approach to removing anticompetitive provisions of state licensing laws. As Miller said, "What the FTC represents is not a vehicle to add government regulation, but a force to root out regulation of the self-imposed sort. That's how you restore a truly free market."[14] Of course, no guarantee exists that such efforts will continue, especially if a new regime with a more hostile attitude toward free markets takes over.

Even if the FTC continues to promote its current deregulatory program, and all indications are that it will, professional groups will continue turning to Congress for relief. These groups have already nearly succeeded in having Congress overturn the commission's right to challenge anticompetitive state licensing rules. The idea, which professional groups are still promoting, is to restrict the federal government's battle against the anticompetitive activities of the professions to the Department of Justice, an agency less aggressive in this area than the current FTC. The Justice Department is concerned primarily with private practitioner activities that masquerade as legitimate state activities.[15] Although differences with state licensing boards are usually resolved before filing suit, a few cases have been brought to trial.

One noteworthy case involved the Texas Board of Accountancy and its ban on competitive bidding. The board asserted the "Parker Doctrine," which the Supreme Court developed in the 1940s to exempt states from federal antitrust law. The Justice Department maintained that because the board's rules became effective after referendum approval by a majority of licensees, the rule could be reviewed as an agreement among Texas accountants to avoid price competition. State law only enabled anticompetitive rules, it did not mandate them. Therefore, the rules should be seen as attempts by private interests, not the Texas state government, to acquire monopoly privileges. A district court accepted the Justice Department's position (later upheld on appeal) and declared the Texas rule to be a per se violation of the Sherman Act.

One hopeful development in the reform movement is the increased involvement of state attorneys general in challenging anticompeti-

---

[14]Warner (1982).

[15]*PRN*, September/October 1984, p. 4.

tive licensing practices. Although many state governments routinely support their licensing boards when antitrust violations are alleged, there are some notable exceptions. Maryland's antitrust division, for example, has implemented a program to encourage licensing agencies to comply with the division's competition policy, avoid antitrust litigation, and alert board members to issues of competition and the effects of regulation. The division issues recommendations to the boards on how best to conform with the program's requirements. If the recommendations are ignored, the division refuses to represent the board in the event of litigation.[16] State attorneys general and licensing boards now cooperate with the FTC on most anticompetitive complaints made by the commission.[17]

**Conclusion**

Individual liberty may be a long-standing American tradition, but it has done little to stem the tide of professional regulation or its control by the professions. Given the historical record, it appears that true reform can come only from the willingness of licensing opponents to meet the challenges posed by licensing advocates in the political, legal, and intellectual arenas.

Primarily, however, licensure is a political process; it has evolved through political activity, and the best hope for reversing it, at least in the short run, rests with political activity. Legal action can help but is expensive, and subject to reversal. Legal trends change, and with so many federal judges nearing retirement, the composition of the federal bench, including the Supreme Court, is likely to undergo significant change over the next decade. How this will affect the future of licensing laws is far from clear.

The reform movement—specifically, the appointment of public members, centralization, and sunset or sunrise review—has been disappointing, and the evidence shows that it is unlikely to become much more effective in the future. The FTC's deregulatory program has met with considerable success, but it must be remembered that the commission's actions are directed at anticompetitive rules. Issues such as training, education, and experience requirements are left

---

[16]*PRN*, May 1985, p. 7.
[17]*PRN*, September/October 1984, p. 3.

to the states to decide. None of the popular reforms, including the FTC's program, questions the fundamental rationale for licensure—the presumed need for government to protect consumers from quacks, incompetents, and frauds.

Certification and other nonintrusive schemes have been shown to afford substantially the same protection to consumers as licensure, but without the cost or violation of basic freedoms. Still, licensure prevails. So long as occupational groups continue to regard restrictive licensing laws both as a crucial element of public recognition and as a certain means of acquiring monopoly privileges, more occupations will demand licensure. Without a countervailing pressure, politicians and government administrators will remain only too eager to supply that commodity.

# References

Akerlof, George A. "The Market for 'Lemons': Qualitative Uncertainty and the Market Mechanism." *Quarterly Journal of Economics* 84 (August 1970): 488–500.

Barger, Melvin D. "Occupational Licensure Under Attack." *Freeman* (April 1975): 195–201.

Beales, J. Howard, III. "The Economics of Regulating the Professions." In *Regulating the Professions*, edited by R. D. Blair and S. Rubin, pp. 125–42. Lexington, Mass.: Lexington Books, 1980.

Begun, J. W. *Professionalism and the Public Interest: Price and Quantity in Optometry*. Cambridge, Mass.: MIT Press, 1981.

Benham, Lee. "The Effect of Advertising on the Price of Eyeglasses." *Journal of Law and Economics* 15 (October 1972): 337–52.

Benham, Lee. "The Demand for Occupational Licensing." In *Occupational Licensure and Regulation*, pp. 13–25. See Rottenberg 1980.

Benham, Lee, and Alexandra Benham. "Regulation Through the Professions: A Perspective on Information Control." *Journal of Law and Economics* 18 (October 1975): 421–47.

Benham, Lee, and Alexandra Benham. "Prospects for Increasing Competition in the Professions." In *The Professions and Public Policy*, edited by P. Slayton and M. J. Trebilcock, pp. 41–45. Toronto: University of Toronto Press, 1978.

Boulier, Bryan L. "An Empirical Examination of the Influence of Licensure and Licensure Reform on Geographical Distribution of Dentists." In *Occupational Licensure and Regulation*, pp. 73–97. See Rottenberg 1980.

California Department of Consumer Affairs. *Professional Licensing in California*. Sacramento: California Department of Consumer Affairs, May 31, 1978.

Carroll, Sidney L., and Robert J. Gaston. "Occupational Restrictions and the Quality of Service Received: Some Evidence." *Southern Economic Journal* 47 (1981): 959–76.

Carroll, Sidney L., and Robert J. Gaston. "Occupational Licensing and the Quality of Service: An Overview." *Law and Human Behavior* 7 (September 1983): 139–46.

Cathcart, James A., and Gil Graff. "Occupational Licensing: Factoring It Out." *Pacific Law Review* 9 (January 1978): 147–63.

Dolan, Andrew. "The Potential of Institutional Licensing and Brand-Name

Advertising in the Medical Care System." *Journal of Contemporary Business* 9 (1980): 35–44.

Dorsey, Stuart. "The Occupational Licensing Queue." *Journal of Human Resources* 15 (Summer 1980): 424–34.

Dorsey, Stuart. "Occupational Licensing and Minorities." *Law and Human Behavior* 7 (September 1983): 171–82.

Evans, Robert G. "Professionals and the Production Function: Can Competition Policy Improve Efficiency in the Licensed Professions?" In *Occupational Licensure and Regulation*, pp. 225–64. *See* Rottenberg 1980.

Federal Trade Commission (Bureau of Economics). "Improving Consumer Access to Legal Services: The Case for Removing Restrictions on Truthful Advertising." Washington, D.C., November 1984.

Freeman, Richard B. "The Effect of Occupational Licensing on Black Occupational Attainment." In *Occupational Licensure and Regulation*, pp. 165–79. *See* Rottenberg 1980.

Friedman, Milton. *Capitalism and Freedom*. Chicago: University of Chicago Press, 1962.

Friedman, Milton, and Simon Kuznets. *Income from Independent Professional Practice*. New York: National Bureau for Economic Research, 1945.

Gellhorn, Walter. *Individual Freedom and Governmental Restraints*. Baton Rouge: Louisiana State University Press, 1956.

Gellhorn, Walter. "The Abuse of Occupational Licensing." *University of Chicago Law Review* 44 (Fall 1976): 6–27.

Greene, Karen. "Number of States Regulating Selected Occupations by Form of Regulation." Typescript, 1983.

Greene, Richard. "Lawyers Versus the Marketplace." *Forbes*, January 16, 1984, pp. 73–77.

Gross, Stanley J. "The Myth of Professional Licensing." *American Psychologist* 33 (November 1978): 1009–16.

Haug, Marie. "The Sociological Approach to Self-Regulation." In *Regulating the Professions*, edited by R. D. Blair and S. Rubin, pp. 61–80. Lexington, Mass.: Lexington Books, 1980.

Hogan, Daniel B. *The Regulation of Psychotherapists, Vol. I*. Cambridge, Mass.: Ballinger, 1979.

Hogan, Daniel B. "The Effectiveness of Licensing: History, Evidence, and Recommendations." *Law and Human Behavior* 7 (September 1983): 117–38.

Holen, Arlene S. "Effects of Professional Licensing Arrangements on Interstate Labor Mobility and Resource Allocation." *Journal of Political Economy* 73 (October 1965): 492–98.

Illich, Ivan. "The Need Makers." In *The Professions and Public Policy*, edited by P. Slayton and M. J. Trebilcock, pp. 341–46. Toronto: University of Toronto Press, 1978.

Isikoff, Michael. "Mustering the Political Will to Deregulate Va. Professions." *Washington Post*, February 7, 1983.

Kane, Michael T. "The Validity of Licensure Examinations." *American Psychologist* 37 (August 1982): 911–18.

Kessel, Reuben A. "Price Discrimination in Medicine." *Journal of Law and Economics* 1 (1958): 20–53.

Kessel, Reuben A. "The AMA and the Supply of Physicians." *Law and Contemporary Problems* 35 (Spring 1970): 267–83.

Klein, Benjamin, and Keith Leffler. "Role of Market Forces in Assuring Contractual Performance." *Journal of Political Economy* 89 (August 1981): 615–41.

Kleiner, Morris M., Robert S. Gay, and Karen Greene. "Barriers to Labor Migration: The Case of Occupational Licensing." *Industrial Relations* 21 (Fall 1982): 383–91.

Lees, D. S. *Economic Consequences of the Professions.* London: Institute of Economic Affairs, 1966.

Leffler, Keith B. "Physician Licensure: Competition and Monopoly in American Medicine." *Journal of Law and Economics* 21 (April 1978): 165–86.

Leffler, Keith B. "Commentary" on Leland's "Minimum-Quality Standards and Licensing in Markets with Asymmetric Information." In *Occupational Licensure and Regulation*, pp. 287–95. *See* Rottenberg 1980.

Leland, Hayne E. "Quacks, Lemons, and Licensing: A Theory of Minimum Quality Standards." *Journal of Political Economy* 87 (December 1979): 1328–46.

Leland, Hayne E. "Minimum-Quality Standards and Licensing in Markets with Asymmetric Information." In *Occupational Licensure and Regulation*, pp. 264–84. *See* Rottenberg 1980.

Lieberman, Jethro K. *Tyranny of the Experts.* New York: Walker and Company, 1970.

Lynn, David S. "Looking Behind the Licensing Laws." Chicago: Heartland Institute, April 24, 1986.

Martin, Samuel. "An Examination of the Economic Side Effects of the State Licensing of Pharmacists." Ph.D. diss., University of Tennessee-Knoxville, 1982.

Maurizi, Alex. "Occupational Licensing and the Public Interest." *Journal of Political Economy* 82 (March/April 1974): 399–413.

Maurizi, Alex. "The Impact of Regulation on Quality: The Case of California Contractors." In *Occupational Licensure and Regulation*, pp. 26–35. *See* Rottenberg 1980.

McChesney, Fred S., and Timothy J. Muris. "The Effect of Advertising on the Quality of Legal Services." *American Bar Association Journal* 65 (October 1979): 1503–6.

Moore, Thomas G. "The Purpose of Licensing." *Journal of Law and Economics* 4 (October 1961): 93–117.

Muzondo, Timothy R., and Bohumir Pazderka. "Occupational Licensing and Professional Incomes in Canada." *Canadian Journal of Economics* 13 (November 1980): 659–67.

National Center for Health Statistics. *Persons Receiving Care from Selected Health Care Practitioners, United States, 1980.* Washington: Government Printing Office, September 1984.

Noll, Roger G., and Bruce M. Owen. *The Political Economy of Deregulation.* Washington: American Enterprise Institute, 1983.

Novak, Michael. *The Spirit of Democratic Capitalism.* New York: Simon and Schuster, 1982.

Office of the Auditor General (California). "Some Continuing Education Courses Do Not Meet State Requirements." August 1984.

Olson, Mancur. "Supply Side Economics, Industrial Policy, and Rational Ignorance." In *Politics of Industrial Policy*, edited by C. E. Barfield and W. A. Schambra, pp. 245–69. Washington: American Enterprise Institute, 1986.

Orzack, Louis H. "International Authority and National Regulation: Architects, Engineers, and the European Economic Community." *Law and Human Behavior* 7 (September 1983): 251–64.

Pashigian, B. Peter. "Has Occupational Licensing Reduced Geographical Mobility and Raised Earnings?" In *Occupational Licensure and Regulation*, pp. 299–333. *See* Rottenberg 1980.

Pauly, Mark V. "The Doctor Drawbridge." *Wall Street Journal*, November 8, 1985.

Pazderka, Bohumir, and Timothy R. Muzondo. "The Consumer Costs of Professional Licensing Restrictions in Canada and Some Policy Alternatives." *Journal of Consumer Policy* 6 (1983): 55–75.

Perloff, Jeffrey M. "The Impact of Licensing Laws on Wage Changes in the Construction Industry." *Journal of Law and Economics* 23 (October 1980): 409–28.

Pfeffer, Jeffrey. "Some Evidence on Occupational Licensing and Occupational Incomes." *Social Forces* 21 (September 1974): 102–11.

Pratt, Leila J. "Occupational Licensing and Interstate Mobility." *Business Economics* 15 (May 1980): 78–80.

[PRN] *Professional Regulation News* (monthly newsletter of the National Commission for Health Certifying Agencies). Various issues.

Rayack, Elton. "An Economic Analysis of Occupational Licensure." Report prepared for the U.S. Department of Labor, 1976.

Rayack, Elton. "Medical Licensure: Social Costs and Social Benefits." *Law and Human Behavior* 7 (September 1983): 147–56.

Relman, Arnold S. "Glut of Doctors Threatens the Quality of Care." *Washington Post*, April 16, 1986.

Rottenberg, Simon. "The Economics of Occupational Licensing." In *Aspects of Labor Economics,* Conference of the Universities-National Bureau Committee for Economic Research, pp. 3–20. Princeton: Princeton University Press, 1962.

Rottenberg, Simon. "Introduction." In *Occupational Licensure and Regulation,* edited by Simon Rottenberg, pp. 1–10. Washington: American Enterprise Institute, 1980.

Rubin, Stephen. "The Legal Web of Professional Regulation." In *Regulating the Professions,* edited by R. D. Blair and S. Rubin, pp. 29–60. Lexington, Mass.: Lexington Books, 1980.

Shepard, Lawrence. "Licensing Restrictions and the Cost of Dental Care." *Journal of Law and Economics* 21 (April 1978): 187–201.

Shimberg, Benjamin, Barbara F. Esser, and Daniel H. Kruger. *Occupational Licensing.* Washington: Public Affairs Press, 1973.

Shimberg, Benjamin. "Testing for Licensure and Certification." *American Psychologist* 36 (October 1981): 1138–46.

Shimberg, Benjamin. *Occupational Licensing: A Public Perspective.* Princeton: Educational Testing Service, 1982.

Stigler, George J. "Imperfections in the Capital Markets." *Journal of Political Economy* 75 (June 1967): 287–92.

Stigler, George J. "The Theory of Economic Regulation." *Bell Journal of Economics and Management Science* 2 (Spring 1971): 3–21.

Trombetta, William L. "The Professions Under Scrutiny: An Antitrust Perspective." *Journal of Consumer Affairs* 16 (Summer 1982): 88–111.

U.S. Department of Health and Human Services (Office of the Inspector General). "Medical Licensure and Discipline: An Overview." Washington, June 1986.

Warner, Margaret Garrard. "Mr. Miller of the FTC Takes on the Doctors." *Wall Street Journal,* August 19, 1982.

White, William D. "The Impact of Occupational Licensure on Clinical Laboratory Personnel." *Journal of Human Resources* 13 (Winter 1978): 91–102.

White, William D. "Dynamic Elements of Regulation: The Case of Occupational Licensure." *Research in Law and Economics* 1 (1979): 15–33.

Williams, Walter E. *The State Against Blacks.* New York: McGraw-Hill, 1982.

Wolfson, Alan D., Michael J. Trebilcock, and Carolyn J. Tuohy. "Regulating the Professions: A Theoretical Framework." In *Occupational Licensure and Regulation,* pp. 180–214. *See* Rottenberg 1980.

# About the Author

S. David Young is on the faculty of the A. B. Freeman School of Business, Tulane University, where he teaches accounting and finance. He is a graduate of The George Washington University and holds advanced degrees from Indiana University (M.B.A.) and the University of Virginia (Ph.D.). His work has appeared in several academic and professional publications.

# Cato Institute

Founded in 1977, the Cato Institute is a public policy research foundation dedicated to broadening the parameters of policy debate to allow consideration of more options that are consistent with the traditional American principles of limited government, individual liberty, and peace. Toward that goal, the Institute strives to achieve a greater involvement of the intelligent, concerned lay public in questions of policy and the proper role of government.

The Institute is named for *Cato's Letters*, pamphlets that were widely read in the American Colonies in the early eighteenth century and played a major role in laying the philosophical foundation for the revolution that followed. Since that revolution, civil and economic liberties have been eroded as the number and complexity of social problems have grown. Today virtually no aspect of human life is free from the domination of a governing class of politico-economic interests. A pervasive intolerance for individual rights is shown by government's arbitrary intrusions into private economic transactions and its disregard for civil liberties.

To counter this trend the Cato Institute undertakes an extensive publications program dealing with the complete spectrum of policy issues. Books, monographs, and shorter studies are commissioned to examine the federal budget, Social Security, regulation, NATO, international trade, and a myriad of other issues. Major policy conferences are held throughout the year, from which papers are published thrice yearly in the *Cato Journal*.

In order to maintain an independent posture, the Cato Institute accepts no government funding. Contributions are received from foundations, corporations, and individuals, and other revenue is generated from the sale of publications. The Institute is a nonprofit, tax-exempt, educational foundation under Section 501(c)3 of the Internal Revenue Code.

CATO INSTITUTE
224 Second St., S.E.
Washington, D.C. 20003